REAL CARIBBEAN PIRATES

Rogues, Scoundrels, Heroes & Treasures

Dan Asfar

FOLK LORE PUBLISHING

The Publisher: Folklore Publishing
Website: www.folklorepublishing.com

Library and Archives Canada Cataloguing in Publication

Asfar, Dan, 1973–
    Real Caribbean pirates : rogues, scoundrels, heroes & treasures / Dan Asfar.

Includes bibliographical references.
ISBN 13: 978-1-894864-69-5
ISBN 10: 1-894864-69-7

    1. Pirates—Caribbean Area—History. 2. Pirates—Caribbean Area—Biography. 3. Buccaneers. I. Title.

F2161.A83 2007   972.9'03   C2007-902319-3

Project Director: Faye Boer
Project Editor: Wendy Pirk
Cover Image: Illustration from *Howard Pyle's Book of Pirates*, Harper & Brothers, 1921, New York, London.

We acknowledge the support of the Alberta Foundation for the Arts for our publishing program.
We acknowledge the financial support of the Government of Canada through the Book Publishing Industry Development Program (BPIDP) for our publishing activities.

Canadian Patrimoine
Heritage canadien

PC: P5

Contents

For Joan and Vaughan, whose time in the Caribbean has not been so harrowing.

~✽~

Acknowledgments

While the niceties of formal acknowledgments might contradict the brutal subject matter contained herein, the author of this volume does not pretend to have much in common with the seafaring demons that plague these pages. Here's to the sorely tested patience of Faye Boer, the editorial touch of Wendy Pirk and the clear blue of Soufriere Bay.

~✽~

Introduction

I WILL TELL YOU OF DIONYSUS, the son of glorious Semele, how he appeared on a jutting headland by the shore of the fruitless sea, seeming like a stripling in the first flush of manhood; his rich, dark hair was waving about him, and on his strong shoulders he wore a purple robe. Presently, there came swiftly over the sparkling sea Tyrsenian pirates on a well-decked ship—a miserable doom led them on.

So begins the 2000-year-old Homeric Hymn to Dionysus, with the Greek god of wine appearing on a shore before Tyrsenian pirates. The pirates, taking note of the young man's good health and luxurious dress, assume him to be a favored son of a wealthy family and take him captive with the hopes of winning a rich ransom. But the bonds the pirates tie him with do not hold. They loosen and fall to his feet no matter how tightly they are fastened, puzzling the marauders. The helmsman takes one look at their captive, sees the "smile in his dark eyes" and immediately understands. This is no rich merchant's son they have taken aboard. He is something else, a being far greater than they—a god. Perhaps even one as mighty as Zeus, Apollo or Poseidon. The helmsman urges his fellow sailors to set their captive free, but his plea is met with laughter and derision.

The master of the ship replies, "Madman, mark the wind and help hoist the sail on the ship: catch all the sheets. As for this fellow we men will see to him: I reckon he is bound for Egypt or for Cyprus or to the Hyperboreans or further still. But in the end he will speak out and tell us his friends and all his wealth and his brothers, now that providence has thrown him in our way."

The helmsman does as he is told, but the pirates do not journey far before the magic of the god of drink seeps into their vessel. Streams of rich wine suddenly sprout from the deck and flow over the ship. A fragrant smell fills the air, and right before the crew's eyes, a thick, flowering ivy winds its way up their mast.

The frightened captain shouts at the helmsman to beach their ship on dry land. But it is too late. The ship belongs to Dionysus now. The capricious god then changes shape, becoming a frightful lion that makes the deck tremble with his roar. To make matters worse, another beast appears, an enormous bear that sprouts from nowhere, like one of the many flowers that are blossoming from the vine.

Cowering together in the stern of the ship, the pirates are paralyzed with fear and wonder. When the lion roars and lunges at them with bared teeth, they act as one, jumping overboard to escape a certain and gruesome end. The moment they touch the water, though, something incredible happens. They are all transformed into dolphins and dart away into the clear blue sea, never to be seen again. Only the helmsman remains aboard the ship. Dionysus grants him mercy.

Surreal, perhaps, like any other Greek myth, the tale of Dionysus and the Tyrsenian pirates is likely one of the oldest pirate stories in Western civilization. Its subject: a crew of Aegean Sea marauders that would have been familiar to audiences of ancient Greece. One of the interesting things about the myth, however, is the familiarity of these Tyrsenian pirates to *our* understanding of the word "pirate," well over 2000 years after the tale was dreamed up.

Like the pirates that occupy the popular imagination today, Homer's crew of Tyrsenians are brash and arrogant in the face of opportunity, callously seizing unguarded fortune when it presents itself. The helmsman is chided when he voices his concern; there is an easy machismo in the pirate captain's reprimand. Yet he and the rest of the crew are quick to flee when the tables are turned and they are no longer the masters of the situation. The theatrics of chauvinistic courage dissolve quickly. And of course, it is noteworthy that of all the gods in the Greek pantheon, it is none other than Dionysus, god of drink, who appears before the pirates, washing their ship in streams of wine, transforming them and their vessel beyond recognition. Even in ancient Greece, it seems, seaborne piracy was thought to be synonymous with excessive drinking. Certainly the Caribbean pirates of this volume did not go anywhere without inviting Dionysus aboard, to the extent that a captain's authority could be seriously compromised once the rum stores were dry and the crew thirsty.

Piracy has been around for as long as there has been cargo to plunder. The Greeks dealt with marauders robbing along the Aegean trade routes. The ancient Phoenicians, famous for their seamanship, produced pirates that ranged over the Mediterranean. To the Roman Empire, the Illyrian pirates cruising the Adriatic were nothing less than "the enemies of mankind." Centuries later, mutually hostile Christian and Muslim corsairs evoked the name of God and Allah in their bloody piratical expeditions in Malta, southern Europe, and up and down the Barbary Coast of North Africa.

And piracy is hardly confined to history. In an unbroken evolution from ancient times, some hell-bent sailors have been engaged in plunder and violence. From the brutal forays of Scandinavian longboats in the European Dark Ages to the modern day marauders who terrorize the waters off the Somali coast and the South China Sea, seaborne piracy has been a constant, universal and international phenomenon among ocean-going people.

Yet given the great historical duration of this ugly activity, it is interesting that today, when most of us think of "pirates," the first image that comes to mind is a specific figure—a cultural icon that finds its roots in a very specific time and place.

Eye-patch. Tricorne. Musket and cutlass. Jolly Roger. Often he has a parrot on his shoulder. He drinks too much rum and is wont to say things like "Matey," "Ahoy!" "Avast!" and, of course, "Arrrrrr!" This pirate is not a rampaging Viking. He is not an Illyrian from the time of Ancient Rome. And he is certainly not a bazooka-toting sailor from the South China Sea.

The unmistakable icon is a partly fictional creation, to be sure—as much a product of the imagination of writers like Robert Louis Stevenson and J.M. Barrie as a portrait of any real-life rum-loving swab that sailed under the sun across the Seven Seas. And the icon has sailed on to the big screen. From Errol Flynn's *Captain Blood* and Burt Lancaster's *Crimson Pirate*, to Johnny Depp's Jack Sparrow, the image of the swashbuckling pirate has enjoyed a long tradition in Hollywood. Part Long John Silver from the pages of *Treasure Island*, part Edward Teach, one-time real-life living terror of the seas under the name Blackbeard, this mythological pirate of popular culture has been created and rec-reated for well over a century.

There is a certain problem that arises with the way history and mythology come together in pirate lore. Having been subject to the creative licence of so many chroniclers, the question of who these men really were has become lost under a century's worth of romantic narration and hyperbolic prose. The serious historian who attempts to write a pirate biography will be con-founded by contradictory information coming from suspect sources. And yet the pirate icon is planted in a very real historical period. He was born in the European colonial period, which began shortly after 1492, when Christopher Columbus sailed into the sparkling blue waters of the Caribbean and claimed the lands he saw for the Spanish Crown, along with all the vast riches it contained.

It ought to be stated that there is no actual claim these pages tell the definitive truth of any of their subjects. The author is more interested in the well-told yarn, in an approximation of the truth that arises from balancing legend with factual account—pursuing the "facts," as they are, all the while aware that the "facts" will only get one so far when studying such mythologized characters. Rather, the author is far more interested in the essence of each pirate's tale, in attempting to get across an idea of who these legendary men might have been in real life.

What follows are the stories of some of the fiercest men produced by European colonialism in the West Indies. These are the real Caribbean pirates— with all their ambition, their greed, their treacherousness and their heroism.

PART ONE

Spaniards, Buccaneers and the First Wave of Piracy in the New World

HIGH SEAS PIRACY IN THE CARIBBEAN followed closely behind Spanish conquest and colonization in the Americas. Word of the immense wealth flowing out of the New World reached Spain's rivals soon after Cortes' defeat of the Aztecs in 1519, but it wasn't until 1523, when a French commander named Jean Fleury inadvertently stumbled on three Spanish caravels on their way back from Mexico, that the rest of Europe really grasped the scale of the Spanish operation. The encounter took place off Cape St. Vincent, and after Fleury's crew apprehended the three vessels, their shocked gasps were heard all the way from London to the palaces of France.

It was a shipment from Cortes, and it amounted to treasure measured in tons: enormous cases of gold ingots, 500 pounds of gold dust, 700 pounds of Aztec pearls, and small mountains of emeralds and topaz. There were gold masks set with precious stones and Aztec rings and coats made from feathers of rare birds. Not long after Fleury intercepted the Spanish ships, Francis I, the King of

France, began doling out letters of marque, official sanctions to attack Spanish ships, to anyone and everyone who owned a ship.

This was when the first age of piracy across the Atlantic began. These first pirates were mainly French, and they made their living by plundering the riches being shipped from the ports of the Spanish Main, the stretch of tropical coastline curving around the southern rim of the Caribbean. Throughout the 16th century and the early decades of the 17th century, the European privateers were based mainly in French and English ports, but after 1620, these budding Empires' excursions into the Caribbean began, and little bases began popping up in the islands. It was the people of one of these early forts who all the pirates sailing in the Caribbean would one day be named after.

The *boucaniers* of Hispaniola, the name given by the Spanish to the island of today's Haiti and the Dominican Republic, were a gang of feral French castaways, settled on the northwestern part of the island. Over the course of many years, they established a crude society, existing right under the noses of the Spanish colonies on the island, illegal and undesirable immigrants who traded their signature smoked meats to passing ships in need of provisions. The Spanish authorities reacted to the offensive presence of these Frenchmen, launching brutal invasions that eventually drove them off the island.

The *boucaniers* were driven out, but by no means defeated. Gathering on nearby Tortuga, a rocky islet about a mile and a half off Hispaniola's coast, they vowed to wage bloody war against all subjects of the Spanish Crown. By 1640, the island of Tortuga had become a thriving pirate stronghold, and the nickname of its residents, "buccaneer," would come to identify any pirate who raided Spanish ships in the Caribbean—be he French, Dutch or English.

Thus the pirates of this era were born. Buccaneers, conducting the bulk of their raids against the Spanish, plundered with the written permission of rival Empires. They were called privateers by the powers that employed them, but this distinction meant little to the Spanish colonists, soldiers and sailors of the West Indies. To them, the buccaneers were pirates, terrorists, ruthless, merciless and bloody.

～◯～

CHAPTER ONE

Sir Francis Drake, The Queen's Pirate

San Juan de Ulúa, 1568:

The Bay of Campeche was still that afternoon, sluggish in the tropical heat that had settled like a thick blanket over the shore, the ships, and the men. Young Francis Drake was on the deck of the *Minion*, looking out over the starboard side. The British flagship was moored within a pathetic cluster of five weatherworn and damaged English vessels. Beyond, a towering fleet of 13 Spanish galleons was poised at the entrance of the harbor. Apparently this was a lucky day; the largest of the Spanish ships was carrying the new Viceroy, Don Martin Enriquez. So said the four emissaries who had just finished delivering their message to the commander of the English expedition, Drake's cousin, Sir John Hawkins.

"Thus, in infinite mercy and indulgence," the leading dignitary concluded, "his Excellency Don Martin Enriquez has seen fit to grant your party safe haven for rest and repair." The man looked down his sharp nose as he spoke, his barely concealed sneer making it clear that he was stooping far too low for his liking in executing this duty for his lord.

He and his entourage wore shining silk over perfectly ruffled white collars, their hair clean and carefully kept, their manicured hands laden with jewels. The four men literally shone under the afternoon sun in obscene contrast to the squalor on the deck of the *Minion*, with its patched sails, storm-battered rigging and the hungry desperation in the lean faces of the crew.

The captain was in no better shape. The noble Hawkins looked more like a half-mad pauper than an agent of the Queen. His beard hung in unruly tangles, while his long-expired finery, threadbare, salt-stained and sun-bleached, bore every mark of over a year at sea. "His Excellency is most gracious," Hawkins said, "but yet grant me a moment of counsel with my officers."

"Of course," said the emissary, nodding and stepping back with his compatriots.

Hawkins bowed stiffly and walked across the deck to the starboard gunwale, where his senior officers were clustered around Francis Drake. Not yet out of his twenties, Drake was one of the freshest faces in the circle of men. His relation to Hawkins had certainly helped him win his commission—the command of the *Judith*, a tiny, 50-ton vessel anchored some 60 yards away. It was an instance where there was wisdom in nepotism, for Drake had quickly distinguished himself as one of the most capable seamen in Hawkins' squadron, emerging as a natural leader in Hawkins' rough fraternity of seaborne officers.

Drake was still meditating on the galleons, appraising with cold eyes the rows and rows of cannons along the galleons' broadsides. *There can be no doubting the terrible firepower of which these great vessels are capable*, he thought, *and yet such prodigious bulk must surely fetter any nimbleness on the wind.*

"What say you, cousin?" Hawkins asked, leaning close to Drake once his officers had crowded around. "I know not if there is any prudence in this business, putting such faith in the goodwill of Spaniards."

"Nay, I should think not," snorted the *Minion's* first officer, a sturdy mariner from Southampton with scars on his forearms and a sunburned face. "Considering the manner in which we've been traveling."

A low murmur of laughter went up from the hardened sailors. "Best not dwell on what shape His Excellency's graciousness would take if he got wind of our happy commerce," said the captain of one of the other English vessels.

Drake's gaze was still fixed on the enormous warships. When he finally spoke, every man bent forward to hear his words: "In sooth, the question of whether or not it behooves us to trust the Spaniards is no question at all. The fact is that we are outmanned and outgunned." He turned to face the men surrounding him before looking to his cousin. "With these odds, surely they have the power to rain destruction at their leisure."

Truth always carries an undeniable ring, and none in the company felt ready to add anything to the young man's observation. No one saw any need to bring up the fact that the mission had not gone exactly as John Hawkins planned it when they set sail from Plymouth over one year ago, in October of 1567. There had been little reason then to predict the dismay and disaster they had since endured.

Hawkins had actually run the exact same voyage two times before: in 1562 and 1564, though never before on such a grand scale. The first leg of the journey was to take the squadron south to the Guinea coast in West Africa, where, with neither mercy nor a single doubloon of human compunction, they would plunder the land for slaves, raiding north and south of the Niger River until their stores were filled to unspeakable capacity with human cargo.

From there, it was across the waters of the South Atlantic to the recently established Spanish colonies in the Caribbean, where they stopped in every port they came across, selling slaves to plantation owners for remarkable profit. Hawkins' 1562 expedition was so successful that Queen Elizabeth lent out the 700-ton *Jesus of Lubeck* to serve as the flagship for his 1564 foray, which ended up dwarfing his first expedition in terms of financial gain.

The Crown was eager to stand behind Hawkins in these ventures, for not only were he and his men making London financiers rich, but they also amounted to a challenge to Spain's jealously guarded monopoly of the vast New World bounty. Thanks to the 1492 voyage of a certain Genoese explorer named Christopher Columbus, Spain was the first European power to plant the crucifix in the Americas. Conquest had begun, and Madrid was quick to assume that everyone and everything they marched over was theirs, an assumption sanctioned by nothing less than divine right, conveniently doled out by none other than the Pope in Rome.

The idea of divine right became a problem after 1517, however, when a German monk named Martin Luther protested Rome's excesses by nailing a sheet of grievances onto the door of a church in Germany. Not long after that, Europe was roiling in the midst of the Reformation, tearing itself apart over the question of who could rightfully claim to represent divine authority on earth. The struggle amounted to nothing less than a redefinition of Christian faith, which, for centuries, had been centered on the authority of the Pope and his priests. What was accepted as "divine" by one camp was labeled profane by the other, and predictably, people found themselves unable to resolve these theological differences peacefully. Anything but. Ambitious princes and kings exploited the religious schism for political gain, and grinding religious warfare between Protestants and Papists became the dominant feature of European politics for the next two centuries.

The Spanish Empire was staunchly in support of the Pope and based its moral authority in the New World on its close relationship with Rome. Yet this moral authority meant little to Protestant sailors, who only saw the stream of riches being moved from the New World to the royal coffers in Madrid. So it was that the early raids of French Huguenots and Protestant Dutch were motivated by a convenient combination of avarice and religious politics. Piratical pioneers, such as the famed Dutchman Louis de Boisot and his French contemporaries Jean Fleury, Jacques Sores and François le Clerk conducted the earliest direct attacks on Spanish shipping. Surprisingly perhaps, given the remarkable talents they would eventually exhibit for the dubious trade, the English were rather slow in picking up on high-seas robbery of this sort, despite the fact that Henry VIII's divorce with Rome also put England at political and religious odds with the Spanish Empire.

Sir John Hawkins' slave smuggling expeditions were actually the first concerted strikes by the English against Spanish hegemony in the West Indies. Not so dramatic as the outright seizure of ships practiced by the French and Dutch, Hawkins' slave trading was based on early economic notions of supply and demand. Spanish colonists proved willing to buy illegally from foreign traders—such as Hawkins—if Spanish merchants proved unable to meet the commercial demands of the colonies.

Because such trade was perceived as enriching Spain's rivals at the expense of imperial coffers, it was forbidden for Spanish colonists to conduct any commerce with foreign merchants. According to the economic thinking of the time, Hawkins' sale of slaves to Spanish plantation owners amounted to Spanish treasure going to London instead of Madrid, where it belonged. So, although Hawkins was not actually boarding Spanish ships and emptying their holds of gold and silver, by smuggling slaves to planters, he was apprehending that gold and silver before it ever saw a Spanish ship.

It was a time when the religious schism between Spain and England was considered just cause for bloodshed. A legitimate English merchant intercepted by Spanish galleons could, at best, expect to pay heavy "shipping duties" or have his goods confiscated. If he was dealing with an overzealous Spanish commander, however, it was entirely possible that he might be branded a heretic against the Church before being summarily executed and then fed to the fish. This was the reception *legitimate* merchants could expect. Needless to say, no English slave smuggler caught in Spanish waters would be foolish enough to dream of a hospitable welcome.

Back on the deck of the *Minion*, Hawkins and his officers were fully aware of this fact as they followed Drake's gaze out to the 13 massive Spanish galleons.

With these odds, surely they have the power to rain destruction at their leisure.

"Aye, that is the humor of it," Hawkins said grimly, inwardly cursing the rotten luck they had endured ever since they struck the Guinea coast. Unlike his previous expeditions, this time around he'd had real difficulty capturing enough men and women to fill his holds. The expedition had spent several months hunting the African coast, being forced more than once to mount risky inland raiding expeditions. It didn't get any better once they passed into the Caribbean Sea. At port after port, they found it next to impossible to unload their cargo on plantation owners who had once been eager to deal. The demand for slaves was still there, but the problem was that the local governors had come under renewed pressure from the Spanish king to reject all commerce with foreign traders.

Hawkins and his men spent the rest of the year under the merciless southern sun, plying the azure waters of the Caribbean, visiting every port on the map, looking for Spaniards willing to buy what they were selling. Supplies were running low. His sailors were beginning to look dangerous. In the end, it took all the haggling, secrecy, negotiation and intimidation Hawkins was capable of to empty his holds.

And then after all of that, when Hawkins had finally completed this brutal commerce and was able to give the happy order—steer north for home—his little flotilla was hit by a series of destructive tropical storms. Enduring one wrathful squall after another, the battered squadron steered blindly through the Gulf of Mexico until they found the curving coastline of the Bay of Campeche. Hawkins' ships moored off San Juan de Ulúa, the treasure port of Vera Cruz, with the order that none of his vessels run their colors. When Hawkins landed with his officers, the port's governor rode out to meet them, assuming they were Spaniards. Instead, the governor found himself surrounded by a gang of ragged and unfriendly looking Englishmen. Hawkins was beyond putting on any gentlemanly airs when he asked the governor if he and his crew could use the port to stock up on supplies and repair their storm-damaged vessels. The governor had no choice but to graciously agree.

Fully aware of the demoralized state of his men and eager to avoid any flare-ups between his sailors and the Spanish, Hawkins sent only a small contingent ashore with orders to set up a cannon platform on high ground, so as to cover the harbor against any approaching enemy warships. The shout went out to the rest of the men: "Begin the repairs and double quick!" No man so much as grumbled over the plethora of orders that went from ship to ship. They worked fast, each man knowing the faster they were done, the faster they could set sail and resume the long-overdue return to England.

But the sun that rose the next day brought with it the same blighted misfortune the crew had been enduring for the last year. "Sail ho! Deadlights a starboard!" came the cry from the crow's nest. Before the morning was up, there were 13 Spanish galleons at the mouth of the harbor—massive warships packed with cannons from fore to aft, with towering stern castles freshly painted and glittering in the day's early light.

Francis Drake was overseeing repairs aboard the *Judith* when the Spanish came into sight. Standing among his men, he tried his best to conceal his awe before the enormous enemy vessels, the smallest among them outweighing his *Judith* by over 300 tons. The order came from Hawkins shortly after: all ship captains were to join him on the *Minion* to parley with the Spaniards.

Drake, Hawkins and the assembled officers on board the *Minion* were not happy to be at the mercy of the Spanish viceroy's good grace, but as Drake had pointed out, they had very little choice in the matter. Thirteen fully equipped warships against their six battered vessels—if it came to a fight, the Spanish did indeed have the power to pulverize them.

Hawkins let out a long sigh, looking from Drake to his officers, to the five battered ships moored around the *Minion*. Sir John Hawkins was an ambitious man—of that there was no doubt. But he was not the sort of man, too common among the British fighting caste, who was so eager for laurels he would march willingly into the jaws of certain death.

Certain death did not sound attractive to the pragmatic Englishman. Not when there were still options.

"Then, good cousin, we would do well to shun any aggravation."

"There will come another day to fight Spain," one of the officers said. "The order of this battle is stacked too heavily against us."

All eyes turned to Drake, but the young commander remained silent, his sharp gaze belying no emotion. He saw no reason to voice the festering doubt that was written all over each man's face.

"So be it," Hawkins sighed. "Let us treat with the Spanish."

"And pray they are good to their word," another man added.

Yet if any man among the English expedition actually prayed that night, subsequent events would suggest that no one was listening. After they received Hawkins' reply that he would honor the Spanish truce, the dignitaries returned to their vessel, and the 13 galleons began moving into the harbor. They were moored next to the English before the sun had set. The heat did not let up through that tense night, which saw hundreds of English sailors sleeping fitfully under the shadow of the Spanish galleons.

Early the next morning, Drake woke to a hissing voice at his door. "Sir, we have received an order that you are to return to the *Minion*. Captain Hawkins requests an audience."

Drake was up, strapping his sword to his waist. "What's the matter?"

"The Spanish, sir. They have been moving armed men from shore to their ships throughout the night."

The sun had not yet risen when Drake rushed out to the *Judith's* deck and scanned the dark shoreline. His eyes narrowed to daggers at the sight. There they were—swarms of boats, perhaps a hundred, cutting through the bay on their way back to port. "Them boats was all full of men on their way out," the night watchman whispered. "Also, look to land. Our gunners on the ground are surrounded."

Drake looked ashore to the elevated position where Hawkins had placed his artillery battery. The cannons were surrounded by a cordon of men in breastplates and plumed helmets. "This does not bode well for us," Drake muttered through gritted teeth. Striding across the *Judith*, he called for all hands on deck, quickly instructing his first officer to take the ship out of the harbor if battle should commence before he was able to return. Then, ordering that a boat be placed in the water, he took five armed mariners with him and began heading back to the flagship.

He would never make it. He and his men were halfway there when the sun peaked over the horizon and the morning's silence was shattered by the thunderous crash of cannons. The Spanish galleons opened fire on the English all at once. Decimation ensued—smoke, fire, torrents of blood and bone on deck. Planks ripped to pieces, masts splintered and sails torn to shreds. Two of the six ships, hit under the waterline, had already begun to sink. And this was but the first volley.

"Back! Back! Back!" Drake shouted over the roaring tumult. "To the *Judith*, or we're all sunk!" He grabbed an oar himself and had just started heaving back to his ship when a screaming cannonball crashed right through the middle of the boat. Two men were killed instantly as the small vessel was ripped in half, and Drake and the surviving mariners were pitched into the sea.

Kicking up to the chaos at the surface, Drake urged his wildly thrashing shipmates to swim for their lives. But one of the great historical ironies of seafaring men is how few of them were able to tread water. Swimming hard through the fiery destruction, Drake was the only man who made it back to his ship. By the time he hauled himself up to deck, his first officer had given the order to weigh anchor and set the sails.

"Evasive action!" came the repeated cry over the whine and boom of harquebus, cannons and musket fire. Everywhere there were bloody, dead and wounded men, blown to bits by shot, felled by musket balls, perforated by crossbow bolts. And yet the *Judith* was still in full action—sailors putting their weight into rigging, mariners on the gunwales firing arrows and musket balls up at the enemy ships. "Sails to the wind! Turn this bucket around!"

Drake saw that his men had not yet succumbed to panic. Sailors were manning their stations, still heedful. And so they were not lost yet. "Men of England!" Drake boomed over the loud din of battle. "I am your captain and swear by God to go down with this ship. But let each swab do his duty, and, God willing, we may yet come out!" He picked a sword off a dead officer on the deck and leapt to the gunwales, jutting his blade at the galleon that was concentrating its fire on them. " All together! Open fire on those fatherless dogs!"

❦

No one knows for certain exactly what transpired in the smoke and chaos of the following hours, only that the English were essentially annihilated. The catastrophic engagement at San Juan de Ulúa was more of a massacre than a battle, where a small group of damaged English ships were caught completely off guard by a vastly superior force and sent to the bottom of the Bay of Campeche. Over 500 Englishmen were killed or captured, and all of the profit that Hawkins had torturously acquired over the last year fell into enemy hands. And yet it was not all death and ashes for the English.

Miraculously, two ships managed to limp their way out of the trap. One was the *Minion*, still commanded by the leader of the ill-fated expedition, John Hawkins. The flagship weathered the concentrated fire of the Spanish force and broke free, albeit at much cost. There were only 15 men left fit to sail after the last cannonball struck, and the journey home was a hellish one for the undermanned, undersupplied, terribly damaged ship.

The other survivor was none other than the *Judith*. Somehow, Drake had kept his men's morale together, and after mounting a vicious counterattack, he managed to weave his tiny ship out of the forest of galleons and into the safety of open water. Drake took a valuable lesson from the engagement, where the *Judith's* speed and maneuverability proved to be a great advantage over the lumbering Spanish galleons. It was a lesson that he never forgot, and it would inform his thinking when he brought ruin to the Spanish Armada.

San Juan de Ulúa was the young captain's first major naval engagement in what would be a long

and legendary career. The memory of the Spaniards' treachery remained with him for the rest of
his days; it filled him with a hot and unappeasable
hatred that would make him into one of Spain's
most feared and reviled enemies. In time, he
became so well known among Spanish chroniclers
of King Philip II's Empire that in written records
of the time, the Spanish often wrote his name as
"Drago," a believed abbreviated form of "dragon."
Needless to say, Drake did not earn the fierce sobri-
quet for having scaly skin or fiery breath, but for
having an incomparable ferociousness and tenacity against his hated adversaries. Thus, while the
Spanish were the undisputed victors at San Juan
de Ulúa, their treacherousness largely made the
man who would become the bane of Spanish
shipping; it put the vinegar in his veins and the
hellfire in his eyes. Drake's fierce leadership cost
the Spanish Crown countless San Juan de Ulúas
in return.

Obsessed by thoughts of retribution, upon his
arrival in London, Drake immediately began planning his vengeance. The plan, which would be
brought to terrible fruition two years later, in
March 1572, was as bold as anything the French
or Dutch had dared against their imperial rival. To
that point, piratical raids against the Spanish had
been mostly limited to taking vulnerable ships in
the Caribbean and the Atlantic. A few bold inter-
lopers had sacked towns such as Santiago de Cuba
and Havana, but mostly, it was unaccompanied

vessels that had the most to fear. The problem, as Drake saw it, was that plunder from such operations would always be limited to the storage capacity of Spanish vessels. Also, the Spanish were becoming increasingly diligent at escorting treasure ships with heavily armed convoys.

Drake's vengeance demanded more gratuitous plunder than any Spanish ship could provide, so he turned his attention to acquiring Spanish treasure *before* it was shipped away. His eyes turned to the ports scattered over the Caribbean coast. During his slave trade expedition with Hawkins, Drake observed that a good many of the Caribbean ports they stopped at along the way had very little in the way of defensive fortifications. Often nothing more than a sprawl of huts situated off a natural harbor, these young settlements often had no walls, minimal artillery and almost nothing for a garrison. Ready, as far as Drake was concerned, for the taking.

With the official backing of Queen Elizabeth, Drake set out from Plymouth on May 24, 1572. He had two small ships, the *Pasco* and the *Swan*, under his command, with a contingent of 73 men, including his brothers, John and Joseph. Having planned his assault with the utmost care and deliberation, he knew his target from the outset. The settlement of Nombre de Dios, a Spanish treasure port on the Isthmus of Darien (modern-day Panama), was a dingy little shantytown of about 200 buildings sandwiched between the Caribbean coast and the edge of the jungle. Hardly the finest town in the Spanish West Indies, it was nevertheless the locus of massive Spanish treasure stockpiles.

Drake had taken a look himself, visiting the town in 1571 disguised as a Spanish merchant. Conducting his own reconnaissance, he took detailed notes of the harbor and the lay of the land, also paying close attention to the King's treasure house and the location of a cove nearby that could provide camouflaged anchorage for a group of ships. He learned that a large portion of the spoils of the Inca Empire came to Nombre de Dios. These riches came from as far away as Bolivia and the mountains of Peru. Massive pack trains traveled thousands of miles to stockpile gold and silver in this inconspicuous settlement. The treasure was transported out by Spanish treasure fleets only twice a year.

Drake also had made a few forays into the surrounding jungle, where he established a relationship with a group of escaped African slaves known as Cimaroons. These transplanted men and women of the South American jungle had little love for the Spanish who had brought them there, and they waged regular guerrilla warfare against their former masters. Of course, Drake would have said nothing about his own previous slaving expedition with John Hawkins and was definitely lucky that none of the escaped slaves roaming the jungles of Darien recognized him. Drake communicated with the Cimaroons because he wanted to know as much as he could about the region he was going into. His strategy did not depend on any sort of alliance, but as Drake well knew after the expedition with John Hawkins, even the best-laid plans had a way of going awry. In such cases, extra friends couldn't hurt.

Drake's party passed by the Gulf of Darien in July of that year, remaining beyond eyeshot of Nombre de Dios and anchoring east of the settlement in the concealed cove Drake had discovered the year before. A contingent of Drake's men got to work cutting down trees and building a primitive fort while the rest began assembling the pinnaces they had packed into their vessels before sailing out. Drake himself was not content to stand around giving orders. When he was not running his men through practice drills for the coming raid, he was heading reconnaissance missions through the countryside to see what the situation around the port was like. During one of these missions, he encountered a group of Cimaroons. The jungle denizens still remembered Drake and greeted him warmly. They informed him that while recent raids by the former slaves had made Nombre de Dios more vigilant to attacks, with more armed townsfolk and a slightly larger garrison, the settlers still hadn't grown wise to the English presence. So far, the expedition could not have gone smoother.

It was a muggy day in early August when Drake and his men packed muskets, bows, swords and powder into their long canoes before pushing out for Nombre de Dios. Sparing only a couple of men to guard the ships while he was away, Drake had 70 men with him as he steered to the site of his much-anticipated vengeance. Seventy men who had sailed across the rough waters of the Atlantic, sweated under the Caribbean sun and slaved away in the mosquito-infested jungles of Darien in preparation for the coming raid. Seventy men who were as eager as their captain for the booty in the Spanish port.

The party hugged the coast as it made its way west, finding moorage at the mouth of the Francisco River just as the last day's light began to fade. There the men waited, going over the details of the raid one final time, until stars crowned the black Caribbean and fireflies flashed in the noisy jungle. A sliver of a moon cast but the faintest glow as the Englishmen pushed their pinnaces off the beach. Under Drake's stern command, none of the men dared raise their voices when they were back on the sea, and they passed silently—the sound of 70-some men barely a whisper on the water.

It was roughly three in the morning when Nombre de Dios came into sight. Piloting their pinnaces at full speed onto the beach, they disembarked quickly and quietly, surprising the single guard who was manning the six-cannon battery on shore. Every man knew his role, and they divided into three groups. The smallest group, consisting of 12 men, guarded the boats. The men fortified the battery, turning the six guns around to face town and fanning out around it, armed with loaded musket, bows and quivers full of arrows.

The remaining men divided into two equal contingents. One, under the command of Drake's brother, John Oxenham, was to go around the western side of town. The second, commanded by Drake himself, was to march straight through Nombre de Dios, taking the central street that emptied onto the waterfront while making as much noise as possible so as to sow panic among the enemy. John's men were to join the cacophony as well, beating drums on their march west of town, creating the illusion that the port was surrounded and beset by a large force. John and his men would wait on the edge of Nombre de Dios until Drake's trumpeter went silent, the signal that it was time to join the attack. The idea was that the two-pronged attack would meet in the center square, where the marketplace and the supposedly treasure-laden governor's house were situated. By then, the port's paltry defense, facing enemies in three areas, would be too confused and panicked to stop the English looting: first the governor's house in the marketplace, and then the King's treasure house off the water.

This was the plan, anyway, as Drake had conceived it over the course of the last year—rethinking every detail in the comfortable confines of his

English study. But there on the Darien coast, in the ungodly heat of the tropical night, Drake was to learn, yet again, how easily a structured plan could unravel.

First, it was not the trumpets and muskets of Drake's men that woke Nombre de Dios. Mere minutes after Drake and his brother shook hands and lead their companies in opposite directions, the port's church bell began to ring. Someone had spotted Drake's company while the men were falling into line at the waterfront, and the alarm was sounded before they were ready. Shouts filled the air as the bleary-eyed militia was roused from sleep.

Drake acted quickly. The element of surprise he had taken such pains to achieve was fading by the second. Drawing his sword, he ran to the head of his hastily formed column. "Now is the time to meet Spain!" he cried. "For England, the Queen and St. George!" A throaty shout went up from the ragged line of men, and with Drake in the lead, they rushed into Nombre de Dios.

The trumpet man blasted away while drummers beat out the march, punctuated by the roar of muskets. Oxenham's men on the edge of town joined the clamor, beating their own drums to their quick step. The effect was just as Drake hoped. Panic seized the Spanish. Sure they were under attack by a large force that had them surrounded, a good number of the locals rushing out onto the streets were not thinking of defense at all, but ran and kept running until they were deep in the jungle.

Yet there were also sturdier men in Nombre de Dios. The quickest among them had been gathering at the church soon after the bell's first peal, and their numbers were swelling by the second. Loading musket and harquebus, fastening bolts into their crossbows, they lined up shoulder-to-shoulder in the marketplace and prepared to meet the force coming down the main street. They did not bother calling out challenges into the darkness when Drake and his men reached the marketplace.

The first English to pour into the marketplace could only make out the dim shape of the Spanish firing line and the smoking fuses of their firearms. In the next instant, the square was lit up by the flash of powder as the roar of gunfire momentarily drowned out the chiming bell. The trumpet call shuddered and died when a musket ball tore through the trumpeter's chest. Several among the first rank of English into the square fell dead or wounded under the withering fire. Drake himself was wounded, shot through the thigh and bleeding badly.

However, no one could tell. Drake shouted at his men to form a line, and his voice did not waver as he called on them to return fire. Neither did his step falter when he ordered the charge, leading his men into the Spaniards who were still standing. The defenders loosed another volley of crossbow bolts and musket balls, and more Englishmen fell. Drake's men hesitated for a moment, the second roar of musket fire impelling them to think twice in the darkness of the marketplace. Exactly how many men were they facing? These Spaniards seemed ready to fight. Maybe Drake overestimated the effect of the racket they were making. Maybe they would all meet their end in this sweaty shanty-town on the edge of the world.

Drake's men might have turned and ran in those crucial moments if they hadn't heard the welcome shout of English voices at the edge of the market-place. Oxenham had signaled the attack when Drake's trumpeter fell, and his men had come running, tearing toward the sound of battle, eager to join the action. Their arrival at the square marked the end of the fight for the Spaniards, who, not so strong as their musket fire suggested, became convinced they were facing an enemy vastly superior in number. They turned and ran, leaving Drake's men in possession of the town center. There was only one Spaniard left in the marketplace, the solitary man in the bell tower.

The church bell continued to ring as the victorious English cheered at the retreat of the Spanish. Drake's boot was filling with blood from the wound in his leg, but he still gave no indication that he had been shot. "We have not decided the battle yet!" he called over the tumult. "Our hands are here to cut Spain's purse, and we must do so quickly."

"Every man knows his position!" Oxenham shouted to his company. "To the governor's house! All haste! And by all that's holy, will one of you swabs silence that infernal bell!"

The raiding party divided again, with one group lighting torches and forming a defensive perimeter around the square, while the other group followed Drake and his brother to the governor's house. Musket fire filled the square as the watchmen opened fire on the bell tower. But the alarm continued to sound as Drake's men forced their way into the governor's house. There was no one there, but a partly saddled jennet next to a lit candle in the courtyard suggested Nombre de Dios' authority had fled in panic. Drake's men stumbled on the booty by the light of their torches, discovering a dark room off the courtyard loaded with silver bars. There was a collective gasp. This wasn't quite a king's fortune, but it was a start.

Drake turned to his men. "Here is the lesser of the two coffers. You must stand on your weapons at this house until we empty the King's treasure house. Do not begin clearing this room until..." Drake would not be able to finish order, for at that moment, the roar of musket and cannon fire tore through the night. Panicked shouts were coming from the marketplace. Drake's stomach tightened as he felt the first lines of his strategy unravel; his attack plan did not include gunfire at this point. "What the devil?"

A breathless sailor came running into the governor's treasure store. "Sir, the pinnaces on the waterfront. They are under attack."

"Impossible," came Drake's shocked response. The Spaniards had been routed from town mere minutes ago. How could they have possibly organized a counterattack so quickly? Another exchange of musket fire sounded, this one closer than the first.

John Oxenham broke the heavy silence in the room. "The town is coming to life, brother. Our time may be running short." Drake turned his back on the silver and strode from the room.

"Every man to shore!" he shouted, emerging from the governor's house. Skittish sailors in the marketplace exchanged potshots with the nearby huts. Drake repeated his order, shouting for every man to head back to the shore. Treasure was one thing, but their boats were their lives.

The men guarding the boats were hard pressed. Musket balls, crossbow bolts and arrows whistled back and forth between the Englishmen on the beach and their largely unseen assailants in the jungle. The sailors manning the battery only managed to loose one volley of cannon fire before being pinned down by concerted fire. Unable to reload the guns, they were reduced to notching and loosing arrows. Things were looking desperate before the main English force arrived, sending a shower of arrows and lead into the edge of the jungle.

The Spanish response was swift and sure, extracting a bloody toll from the English reinforcements as they scurried for cover. Immediately, the now limping Drake realized that, for all his preparation, he had made a major error. The men in the jungle were not regrouped militia. The residents he had just driven from the marketplace were certainly still fleeing from their embattled town. The men he was facing off against now were professional soldiers. It was obvious by the speed and accuracy of their fire. From where he was, he could hear the clipped orders and curt replies and could see the glint of breastplate and helmet against the flashing guns.

Things had changed in Nombre de Dios since Drake's last conversation with his Cimaroon friends. The garrison had grown dramatically since then, being very recently bolstered by the addition of 150 Spanish soldiers sent down to deal with the constant Cimaroon raids. These men were dug in at the edge of the jungle, keeping a steady fire on the English. Drake's force was pinned down on the shore of an enemy port without a single piece of silver in their hands nor any concrete plan of how to get one.

Drake refused to accept the situation. The empty boats beckoned, but he simply did not have it in him to retreat and give up on the raid, not after everything he and his crew had gone through. And then there was the shame of returning to England empty-handed. No. The Spanish force was not standing between him and the King's treasure house. If he and his men acted quickly, they would still be able to make a run for the loot before pulling out.

Falling in to where the bulk of his men were taking cover, Drake announced his intention. "There are enough of us to keep the Spanish at bay and seize the treasure house. Yet we must be swift, lads, 'ere the townsfolk rally and return to the fight." John Oxenham, crouched close to Drake, was the first to notice that something was wrong with his brother. Drake's face was pale, and his breath was labored.

One of his sailors spoke up. "I wonder, sir. Is this too much ambition? Every man here is loathe to leave empty-handed, but forces be conspiring against us."

It was not so uncommon for 16th-century sea-men to question their captains. Military hierarchies that were already so well established in the army had not yet been entrenched in the Royal Navy. Indeed, most of the men under Drake's command were civilians, perceiving themselves to be sea-faring men rather than soldiers of the crown. It was a part of Drake's station to convince his men that his orders were not leading them to certain death.

"And what forces would those be, man?" he replied. "A loose gathering of savage Popish idolaters in the trees? Let us not lose our mettle, not when the Spaniard's treasure is so near." Drake pointed at a structure on the beach, some 40 yards away—the King's treasure house. As Drake said, the English were already dug in between the Spanish on one side and the storehouse on the other. "There it is. We need hold here only long enough to empty the store."

Another round of fire tore up the sand around them, and Drake could see the dim outline of his men under the starry sky. He could feel the dubious glances in the darkness. He drew himself up to his full height, and though was not a tall man, he was broad enough in the shoulders to present the enemy with a tempting target.

"By Jove, sir!" one of the crouching sailors called. "You will get yourself killed!"

It was then that Drake delivered the words that have lived on in every recounting of the raid on Nombre de Dios. "I have brought you to the treasure of the world," he said. "If you leave without it, you may henceforth blame nobody but yourselves."

Just in case this was not motivation enough, John Oxenham decided to add some words of his own. "You heard the man, you cowardly swabs! I did not cross over half the world to turn and run empty-handed. Now stand your ground! And by

God, I swear to cut open the first man who shows his back!" Oxenham's addendum tipped the scales. Motivated to hold on a little longer, the majority of the force continued to exchange fire with the soldiers, while a smaller detachment, lead by Drake, bolted to the treasure house.

By this point, it had become fairly obvious that Drake was hurt. His voice had lost its commanding timber, and he was limping noticeably. Whenever he stood still for any length of time, blood filled his footstep in the sand. John grabbed him moments before the dash for the treasure house began. "You are wounded, brother. It may be for the best if I lead the run."

Drake jerked free of his brother's grasp. "Just hold here for a little longer. We will return in good time." He called to his men, and Drake's small company dashed across the beach at a running crouch.

Oxenham swallowed hard and turned his attention to the enemy in the jungle. He could not tell how many men they were facing, but there was reason to worry. It had begun to rain moments after Drake departed. More and more of his men were discarding muskets for bows as they ran out of ammunition, and Oxenham knew as well as anyone that wet bowstrings would be about as useful as a fistful of sand in a fight. Furthermore, there was movement in the streets of Nombre de Dios.

The militia had rallied sooner than expected and were gathering themselves together to rejoin the fray. The British were holding up against the soldiers in the jungle, but Oxenham knew they would be quickly overcome if the militia mounted an attack. Even worse, there was a possibility that the Spanish had cannons in town and were moving them into position. It was also possible that the Spanish were moving from the jungle into town in a bid to outflank them. Drake's carefully planned raid seemed to be on the verge of collapse. Everywhere he looked, Oxenham saw defeat. And yet it did not come that day. Before John Oxenham was able run any more dismal scenarios through his head, his brother's company had returned. They had taken almost no time at all, and it was immediately obvious that something was very wrong.

White as death and laboring heavily for each breath, Drake could barely stand any longer, and his wounded leg was now covered in blood. But the worst thing was the expression on his face. It was not agonized, but numb, stunned, defeated. "What happened?" said Oxenham.

"There is no treasure," Drake said. "They have emptied the storehouse. There is nothing there. Not a single doubloon." He collapsed onto the sand next to his brother as the rain picked up to a torrent. "The fleet must have already arrived for it. We are too late."

The wound to his leg he had endured, but the collapse of his plan proved too much to bear. Oxenham, now, was focused solely on survival. "Then we must go, Francis. Sound the retreat. Our weapons are useless in this deluge, and the town militia is mobilizing. All is lost if we linger for much longer."

But it was too much to ask of Francis Drake. He simply could not accept a failure of this magnitude. He dragged himself back to his feet. "There is still silver in the governor's house!" he shouted. "One more foray into the marketplace! It must be done!"

It was the last order Drake gave that night. The world tilted as soon as he got up; he staggered once and then collapsed. He had lost too much blood. And yet even as he lay trembling on the sand, barely holding on to consciousness, he tried to protest as his officers sounded the retreat. He felt hands hauling him up by his arms and dragging backward across the beach to the pinnaces. His eyes were fastened on Nombre de Dios as the Spanish soldiers rushed from the jungle and the militia came streaming out of town. There were shouts and curses as he was dragged into the water. And then the world went black.

When Drake came to days later, he woke in a camp that was practically unrecognizable. Everything had changed. Limping among his men, he saw defeat written on every face. Nursing their wounded and grieving their dead, the men languished in idleness and despair. Very few of these men shared their leader's extreme fervor for Queen and country; at heart, they were sailors, privateers, who had committed themselves to Drake with the understanding that there was booty to be had at the end of the journey. Now the prospect of no loot, after all they had sacrificed, was too much to bear.

Since the return from the failed raid, no one had the will to determine the next course of action. Instead, the men set about consuming all the liquor they had in their ships' holds, immobilized by heat, alcohol and general malaise. No one was looking forward to returning to England empty-handed. And yet, after the disaster of the failed raid, none of them were eager to continue on in the West Indies, either.

What followed says much of Drake's inherent ability as a leader among men. After one bottle-strewn walk through the demoralized encampment, he called the sailors together and spoke his mind. After he was done, the men were back on their feet, cleaning the beach of the refuse they had strewn about over the last few days, preparing themselves for the next course of action. They were ready for plunder once again.

Perhaps it was the fact that Drake drew his motivation from loftier sources. Never purely inspired by wealth alone, Drake was a fiercely religious man who saw no issue linking his Protestant beliefs to the political designs of Elizabethan England. Drake went through his world with a hard light in his eyes and an unmistakable proficiency with his hands. A sailor, privateer and explorer guided by forces few men felt, he was what others called inspirational. With a few words, he was able to turn his discouraged rabble into willing fighting men once again.

Not that the coming months would be easy. The men stayed on in the southwest corner of the Caribbean, seizing what ships they could in the Gulf of Darien while launching minor operations along the coast. Initially, Drake had his eye on other treasure ports, and he flirted with the idea of raiding Cartagena, but the attempt at Nombre de Dios had dulled his ambition. Deciding that he did not have the manpower to mount such a raid, Drake focused on more modest objectives, taking smaller ships, concentrating on seizing supplies to keep his operation going, keeping his eyes open for *the opportunity*—the one raid, the one chance, the one strike at riches that he promised his crew. He urged patience, perseverance and discipline. The opportunity would arise.

In the meantime, he fostered closer ties with the Cimaroons. They began coming down from the jungle regularly, trading supplies and information for English tools and weapons. They helped the sailors construct sturdier houses in their encampment. Most importantly, they became firm allies in Drake's operations against the Spanish.

It was through the Cimaroons that he learned about the silver train that came seasonally across the isthmus. This train, he was told, moved east after the rainy season, carrying silver mined from Peru to the treasure ships waiting at Nombre de Dios. Told that these laden caravans were sent along narrow trails through thick jungle, Drake sensed that the opportunity had finally arrived.

The problem was timing. The treasure fleet always arrived after the rains, and the mule trains never started their journey until there were ships docked at Nombre de Dios. This meant Drake and his men would have to say put for the next several months. It was a lot to ask.

Restlessness was not the only ailment that beset his seamen. A few sailors had fallen ill—bedridden, aching and feverish, breaking out in jaundiced splotches all over their bodies. Yellow fever, the tropical plague, had already begun to move among the men. It would only get worse with time; the jungle, they knew, could kill them. Nevertheless, history had proven time and again that, where men of the sea are concerned, the lure of glory and booty trumps the risk of death almost every time. The following months sorely tested the limits of what Drake and his men could endure.

Death came from every angle. Yellow fever spread through the camp. Raids for supplies on passing Spanish vessels brought casualties. Over 28 men died in battle with Spanish vessels. In the fall of 1572, John Oxenham himself was shot to death while leading a boarding party. Drake's other brother, Joseph, died of yellow fever in January 1573. Weeks passed in which even Drake's indomitable will began to falter under the deluge of the rainy season, as swarms of mosquitoes and unrelenting heat hung over the dismal camp. Finally, a Cimaroon party came to his camp with welcome news. A treasure fleet had landed at Nombre de Dios; a mule train was on the march.

It was said there were 14 mules laden with gold, silver and jewels and that they were accompanied by only a small escort. Finally, it seemed, fortune was smiling on Drake. Invigorated by the news, Drake took 15 men with him and set out behind a group of Cimaroon guides. Weighed down by their weapons and supplies, the men labored through the claustrophobic swelter of the jungle, driven on by visions of vast booty. Drake's tired steps were surely fueled by this very same vision; until, that is, February 11, 1573, when Drake's life was changed forever.

They had been hiking for 12 days when they came upon a ridge crowned by enormous trees. The head scout stopped the party at the foot of the mountain, telling Drake the top of the ridge offered a grand vantage of the surrounding country. Was he interested in taking a look at the ground they had covered? Naturally curious about the lay of the unmapped land, Drake told the scout to lead the way, and up they went as the rest of the company took a rest.

The Cimaroons had made one of the trees into a primitive watchtower, cutting small steps up its base until it was possible to use the branches to climb all the way to the top, where they had made a small observation post. After so many days in the confines of the jungle below, Drake could not have been more stunned by the view.

There, to the west, was a sparkling, immense expanse of water stretching out as far as the eye could see. It was the Pacific Ocean, or as it came to be called then, the South Sea. Drake was the first Englishman to lay eyes on it. Uncharted water, undiscovered country—the idea made something surge within him. The fire of new ambition was lit, and Drake vowed to himself that he would return one day to sail those uncharted waters. He climbed back down into the close heat of the jungle, fortified by what he had seen and looking beyond the misery he and his men had endured on this expedition. Still, it was barely enough to get him beyond the next disappointment.

One week later, he and his men were positioned in the bush around the narrow trail between Panama and Nombre de Dios, waiting in ambush for the mule train heading for the treasure port on the northern coast. The English and the Cimaroons were crouched in the jungle on either side of the road. Drake had his men wearing bright white shirts so that they would easily be able to spot one another if there came a need for shooting. But for now, they were all invisible, lying low in the dense foliage.

Two Cimaroon scouts rushed up to Drake, whispering that a mule train was approaching from the south, bound for Nombre de Dios—14 mules, just as they had heard, loaded with bullion and guarded by a dozen or so Spanish soldiers. It would be arriving any time. No sooner had Drake received the hissed report than mule bells were heard coming down the trail. The problem was that the bells were approaching from the north, the wrong direction.

A confused buzz sounded among the English as a Cimaroon dashed off to investigate. He was back minutes later. "These men are coming from Nombre de Dios," he hissed to Drake. "They carry no gold or silver, only tools and weapons for Panama."

Drake did not waste a moment. "Pass the word. No one is to fire on the train approaching from the north. It carries nothing of value. Remain in hiding until it passes. The train from the south is our target." The order was passed quickly from one man to the next as the first beast of burden rounded the northern bend. A Cimaroon warrior from Drake's side of the trail gave a signal to a Cimaroon hidden on the other side, and the word was whispered among the men.

It was a close thing, but every man had heard the order by the time the first mule labored by. The raiders lay flat on their stomachs, holding their breath, watching the train pass. Through the bush, they could see the hooves of one mule, then two, then three, accompanied by the leather boots of Spanish soldiers and the unclad feet of slaves.

Disaster struck by way of the sheer stupidity of a man by the name of Robert Pike. Pike had packed a bottle of wine at the outset of the journey, thinking he could use extra courage when the time to fight came. Unfortunately, he had imbibed too much of it while he lay waiting, so he was well past brave and into witless by the time the mule train passed by. Pike heard the order to sit still from the man lying next to him, but he did not think it particularly important. Perhaps he decided that it would be an admirably brave thing to confront the Spanish train alone. With his bright white shirt and his musket clasped in a hand that hung limply at his side, Pike stood up and hollered his challenge. "Right then, what do you bloody Spanish think you're up to?"

Hell immediately broke loose. The four or five soldiers guarding the caravan turned their weapons on the man, shouting at the mule drivers to speed their beasts ahead. The drunken Pike fired his musket wide of any target before diving to the ground in terror as the Spanish drew their swords and rushed forward. Panicked shouts erupted when they crashed into the bush and found themselves surrounded. There was more musket fire, and two of the soldiers fell dead while the rest surrendered where they stood. The mule drivers raised their hands, and the swarming English and Cimaroons promptly apprehended the supply train.

The whole affair was over in a matter of seconds, but it was loud enough to alert the treasure caravan that had been approaching from the south. The captain of the guard, a cavalry officer, galloped up the trail to investigate. Catching sight of the white shirts through the trees, he promptly spun around and galloped back, ordering the train back to Panama and bringing his soldiers up to a defensive position as the 14 treasure-laden mules made their getaway. Drake did not have any choice but to let them go. A frontal assault on the dug-in soldiers would be suicide. And now that the Spaniards were aware of the presence of Drake and his men, the mule trains coming through would certainly be accompanied by heavy escorts, which would be too much for 15 Englishmen and an equal number of Cimaroons to take on.

And so they began the three-week march back to their camp, exhausted and empty-handed, but for the pots, pans, swords and muskets they seized from the southbound caravan. The haul was nothing less than a mockery to the English's aspirations, yet the Cimaroons were ecstatic. Having no use for gold and silver in the fight against the Spanish, the Cimaroons valued the steel tools and weapons of their former masters far more than any glittering metal dug out of the ground.

The heartbreaking disappointment of the group's return to the camp would have certainly marked the lowest point of an expedition which had already had too many losses. With their numbers whittled by combat and disease, living for months out of huts on a mosquito-ridden stretch of sand with nothing but each other for company, did the men begin to whisper of mutiny? One thing seemed certain—rebellion against their stubborn commander was beginning to look like the only way they might ever see the cliffs of Dover again, unless they could win the plunder that had eluded them for the better part of a year.

It did seem that every defeat only hardened Drake's resolve. With the unearthly tenacity he would become famous for, Drake regularly evoked the Queen, God and their lost comrades when making his rounds, assuring his men that it was quite impossible to turn around now, given everything they had sacrificed. No one could deny that Drake suffered as much, or more, as any of the men had, having lost two of his brothers, enduring the same daily privations and facing the same dangers. Perhaps it was Drake's unbending stoicism in the face of such difficulty that shamed the sailors into obedience. Whatever the case, they remained loyal, holding to their captain, who continued to declare that God was on their side and that those who suffered always reaped the greatest reward.

When good fortune finally did arrive, it came in March 1573 by ship, borne by a hard-nosed Huguenot freebooter named Captain Testu. Hailing from the French port of Le Havre, Testu had been sailing the Caribbean bearing a letter of marque to attack Spanish ships. Drake and Testu shared the same enemy, and the French were warmly welcomed in the English camp—at least as warmly as the demoralized and disease-ridden English were able. But when Testu informed Drake that he knew the whereabouts of three enormous treasure caravans that were currently bound for Nombre de Dios, the welcome went from warm to familial. No less than 190 mules, Testu said. He was looking for safe moorage as close to the treasure port as possible, where his men could disembark and raid the caravans in the jungle outside of town. Their only concern was the escort, which was a sizeable guard. "Monsieur Drake, would you care to join forces in this enterprise?" asked Captain Testu. It might very well have been the stupidest thing the privateer ever said.

It was 1573 and rum would not be distilled for roughly another 80 years. So the French and English sailors made do the with copious stores of wine plundered from the Spanish, dissolving centuries-old antagonisms in the waters of the New World. Not only was Drake able to direct Testu to the best mooring spot near Nombre de Dios, he was also able to call on the support of the Cimaroons. It is not known exactly how many Cimaroons joined the raid. Always ready to make things difficult for the Spanish, the escaped slaves probably contributed roughly one-third of the force, somewhere between the 15 English and 20 French fighting men partaking in the ambush.

So it was a combined force of some 50 French, English and African men that sailed east along the coast. Directed by Drake, they piloted their vessels up a river close to Testu's proposed ambush site. They hid their vessels along the riverbank and hiked inland, setting up their reception for the Spanish some 20 miles from Nombre de Dios.

They slept about a mile from the trail that night, waking the next morning with Cimaroon scouts reporting the approach of Spanish caravans. Captain Testu's information had been accurate. Three caravans with nearly 200 mules buckling under enormous saddlebags approached. There were also about 50 Spanish soldiers escorting the train.

This time, however, there was no inebriated Robert Pike acting on wine-fueled delusions of grandeur. This time there was no hint of movement, no rustle, no whisper, no breath that warned of the sudden roar of musket fire that erupted in the jungle. The Spanish soldiers that survived the opening volley returned fire, but their panicked response, shot blindly into the jungle, was ineffective. In the next moment, the jungle came to life with multilingual oaths and battle cries as Frenchmen, Englishmen and Africans rushed the soldiers with their swords, spears, axes and clubs.

The battle did not last long. The Spanish were taken completely by surprise. Those who did not flee outright stuck around just long enough to ask themselves if they'd done enough to earn their soldiers' salaries. One look at the mad faces of their desperate and tattered enemy convinced them that they had done their duty. Firing off whatever weapons they had, they turned and ran for the safety of Nombre de Dios.

As the smoke from the brief engagement crept into the jungle, Drake and his 15 Englishmen, standing next to their French and Cimaroon allies, found themselves in possession of more loot than any of them had ever seen in their lives. Each of the 190 mules was loaded with about 300 pounds of silver. There were also several chests filled to bursting with gold doubloons. Finally, after all the dismal failures, this was the raid the pirates had been waiting for. They consented, at last, to raise sails and head back to England.

The victory did not come without cost, however. A few men had been hit by the Spaniards' panicked fire. Captain Testu was among them, writhing on the ground with a musket ball in his stomach. The Huguenot sailor stayed alive for a few more hours, finally breathing his last as the men loaded the treasure onto their boats. After a few words, they left Testu's body in the jungle by the treasure he had found but would never be able to spend. There was too much gold and silver to carry on their boats, and the men buried it next to the French captain's body. Drake actually did make an attempt to come back for the booty a few days later, only to find it had already been dug up by the Spanish.

Not that he or his men were in need of anything extra. Of the 73 that set out, only 30 were still alive. Thirty men brought home what amounted to about 15 tons of silver ingots and over £100,000 in gold currency. After a year at sea, Drake and his crew arrived in Plymouth on August 9, 1573, all wealthy men.

Yet this was not the end of Drake's career. A staunch patriot, he would spend most of his life on the prow of a ship, flying the flag of Saint George from his mastheads, heaping glory on the Crown and visiting grief on Queen Elizabeth's enemies. In December 1577, four years after returning from Nombre de Dios, he set out on the voyage that had been inspired by his glimpse of the Pacific Ocean on the Isthmus of Darien. It would arguably be Drake's greatest accomplishment. At the head of five ships, which would quickly be reduced to one, he sailed around the world, taking the Strait of Magellan and heading north up the Pacific side of the Americas. He attacked every Spanish vessel he encountered along the way, looting up and down the west coast until the waters were teeming with Spanish galleons hunting for him. Drake then turned west, crossing the Pacific Ocean, through the islands of Indonesia, rounding Cape Good Hope, returning to Plymouth on September 26, 1580. Surviving storms, boardings, attacks by island natives and an attempted mutiny, he returned in great fanfare, the holds of his ship bursting with Spanish loot. The expedition marked the second time, after Magellan, that anyone had circumnavigated the globe. But unlike Magellan, Drake survived the journey, winning the distinction of being the only commander to complete the trip. Queen Elizabeth herself knighted him on the deck of his ship.

Even then, Sir Francis was not done winning laurels. In 1587, he oversaw a major raid of the Spanish harbor of Cadiz, destroying 30 enemy ships in the process. A year later, when King Philip decided he'd had enough and mobilized the Spanish Armada to invade England, Drake was appointed the vice-admiral of the British fleet. Because of what he had learned of the lumbering Spanish galleons during his many encounters with them, Drake played a major part in the defeat of the Armada, with his swift maneuvers and bold attacks.

A national hero, famous navigator and legend-ary privateer, Drake made his name on the undis-covered waters of the 16th century. He was born with only modest connections to English gentry, but by the end of his illustrious career, every British subject knew his name, and he had the ear of none other than the Queen of England. English histori-ans hesitate to place Drake among the depraved pantheon of robbers that terrorized the seaways. Yet to the Spanish, this was precisely what he was—a God-fearing, honorable and patriotic robber, but a robber nonetheless.

And while his appointment as a vice-admiral would be considered a blot on any piratical resume, Drake's adventure in and around the Isthmus of Darien in 1572 and 1573 would become something of a blueprint and inspiration for the buccaneers of the coming century. Any pirate facing an impos-sible situation on the sultry waters of the Carib-bean needed only to remember the brutal odyssey that Sir Francis Drake came through after the raid of Nombre de Dios. He would go down as the inspi-ration, the patron saint, the guardian angel of every cutlass-waving swab that preyed on Spanish ships in the West Indies.

It is fitting, then, that the West Indies is where his remains were laid. Unlike the grand achieve-ments of his life, death came squalidly and insidi-ously to Francis Drake. He set out on his last expedition in August 1595, once more to the

Caribbean, once more in the company of his cousin, Sir John Hawkins. The scope of this mission was much grander than the slave trading expedition of 1567. Queen Elizabeth gave them a flotilla of 26 ships with orders to sail to Puerto Rico to capture a damaged treasure ship moored in the port of San Juan, while sowing whatever destruction they could on Spanish shipping.

Everything went wrong. By the time they arrived in Puerto Rico, the treasure ship they were after had been well fortified in San Juan. Deciding to conduct raids along the Spanish Main, Hawkins and Drake sailed their fleet for the island of Dominica, where they stopped to careen their vessels. In late October, in the waters off the tiny volcanic island, Sir John Hawkins caught a fever and never recovered. The venerable English seaman succumbed to his sickness on November 12.

Drake carried on but was heartsick at the loss of his cousin. He set sail for Nombre de Dios, intent on using the port as a base to strike at Panama and Porto Bello, hoping, perhaps, to replicate his earlier success on the Isthmus. That success never came, and early in 1596, Drake contracted a virulent case of dysentery. He remained sick and feverish in his quarters for three weeks, until the disease finally claimed him on January 28, about a mile off the town of Porto Bello. The next day, his men placed his remains in a lead coffin and sealed it tight. A mass was given, followed by a solemn recital of the great seaman's august achievements. The venerable Admiral's coffin was then thrown overboard and sank straight to the bottom of the bright blue waters.

CHAPTER TWO

The Three Campaigns of Henry Morgan

ONE MIGHT BE TEMPTED TO SAY that Henry Morgan picked up where Sir Francis Drake left off, for it was at bustling Porto Bello in 1668, over 70 years after Drake's coffin was sent to the bottom of those same waters, that Henry Morgan launched the raid that inaugurated his blood-soaked career. On one hand, it was yet another attack on a Spanish treasure port by an English privateer, reminiscent of the same raids Drake had launched so many years ago. On the other hand, nothing Drake had ever done in the Caribbean matched the scale or savagery of Morgan's Porto Bello attack—or any other of his raids, for that matter. The West Indies had changed a great deal in the three-quarters of a century since good old Francis Drake was laid in the arms of Davy Jones.

While the Spanish were still the dominant power in the Caribbean, years of Dutch, French and English aggression had whittled away much of their monopoly in the Americas. In Drake's time, the population in the West Indies was made up of indigenous groups alongside a relatively small number of Spanish colonizers in the ports that dotted the coastlines. Raids on Spanish ships and colonies were based from European ports, and the Atlantic saw heavy traffic, with privateer fleets constantly moving between the Atlantic and the Caribbean, plundering waters from cities such as St. Malo, Le Havre, Amsterdam and Plymouth.

This began to change in the early decades of the 1600s. French, English and Dutch colonies began popping up on the Leeward and Windward Islands, the archipelago of small islands that marked the eastern boundary of the Caribbean. French patents granted by Louis XIV saw colonies spring up in Martinique and Guadeloupe just as the British Crown authorized the occupation of Barbados, Nevis, Montserrat and Antigua, while the Dutch seized Saba, St. Martin, St. Eustatius and Curaçao. Slaves and indentured servants made up the bulk of early settlers, clearing the ground for the sugar plantations that would come to dominate the landscape, while pirates and privateers began to use these young colonies as launching points for their attacks on the Spanish.

The number of inhabitants on these islands swelled in the following years, so that by 1654, the year Cromwell launched his religious grand design to capture Hispaniola from the Spanish, roughly 6000 of his 7000-man army were recruited from the restless and rootless young men of Barbados, St. Kitts and Nevis.

Henry Morgan's early years are not well documented, though it is generally accepted that he did nothing of note in his native land. One version of his story counts him among the men who set out from England with General Venables and Admiral Penn in the name of military conquest. This claim has been disputed, however, most notably by Alexander Exquemelin, famed pirate chronicler of the time, who himself served under Morgan in later raids. In his seminal book, *The Buccaneers of America*, written in Dutch and subsequently translated to English and French, Exquemelin claimed that Henry Morgan was the son of a yeoman farmer and that he began his career in the West Indies rather humbly, as an indentured servant in Barbados.

Exquemelin's book was published in 1678 and was an instant success with European readers intrigued by the unsavory characters who ruled the waves on the edge of civilization. Morgan, however, was enraged by his portrayal. By that time he was living high as the pre-eminent buccaneer of the West Indies, feared and respected among Caribbean pirates and English elites alike. It says a great deal about Morgan's character that in a biography that painted him as a merciless beast prone to brutal torture, senseless destruction and wanton rapine, he was most angered by Exquemelin's claim that he had come to the West Indies as an indentured servant. Furious at the perverse suggestion that he came from humble origins, he sued the publishers of the English version of the book for libel, insisting that he was, in fact, "a gentleman's son," and that he "never was a servant to anybody in his life, unless to his Majesty."

Whatever his origins were, Morgan was undeniably a man of great ambition, bent on improving his lot in the rigid hierarchy of the Old World. A man so obsessed with social climbing would have seen nothing but opportunity in the free-wheeling violence and volatility of the West Indies, and his incredible ascent in that rough and unruly world is clear evidence of how well he seized these opportunities.

History is full of ambitious men; indeed, the vast majority of leading men among our buttoned-down elite might be described as relentless climbers painfully jealous of their reputations. Yet there was more to Morgan than brazen ambition. He proved to be an able leader in the chaos of the Caribbean's piratical milieu because the same chaos reigned within him. A heavy drinker who lived for rough carousing with his fellow seamen, he was possessed of the same vigorous appetites that pushed so many other rootless men to the sea: a thirst for freedom, adventure, rum and riches— driven by dreams of hard courage, vanquished enemies and glittering booty. In short, Morgan rose to the top of the buccaneer hierarchy largely because he himself was the embodiment of the ideal. He was a man without fear or compunction, utterly unabashed and immoral in his pursuit of gold and glory.

Whether a pauper or an officer, this terror-in-the-making was set loose in the West Indies in 1654, one of some 7000 souls under the command of Venables and Penn, bound for Santo Domingo on the south shore of Hispaniola. The operation was a complete debacle; losses from Spanish muskets, cannons and tropical disease sent the expedition back to their ships, where it was determined that they could not sail back home without conquering something.

So they turned their lusty eyes to the island of Jamaica. Not nearly as populated as Spain's coveted Hispaniola, the smaller island was guarded by a tiny Spanish force, which was easily overwhelmed by Venables and Penn's superior numbers. Something of a consolation prize after the failure at Hispaniola, Jamaica would become one of England's most important possessions in the Caribbean, providing an invaluable base for Royal Navy and privateer excursions against the Spanish.

The newly acquired island came to be considered the southern point of the Tortuga-Jamaica piratical axis that would torment Spanish interests in the Caribbean for decades to come. The tiny island of Tortuga, off the northwest coast of Hispaniola, had been providing safe haven for pirates for over 20 years when the British landed in Jamaica. The first inhabitants of the famed island were the original "buccaneers," a name derived from those early inhabitants' practice of cooking by *boucan*, a process adopted from local natives which involved smoking meat over dung and wood-chips.

Originally from the north coast of Hispaniola, the peculiar subculture began sometime in the 1500s, as passing French, Dutch and English smugglers and privateers took up the habit of marooning undesirable crewmembers on the island. Decades saw this group of castaways flourish right under the nose of Spanish authority. Making a living hunting wild pigs and selling provisions to passing ships, the castaways grew into peculiar ways. They formed a male-dominated society that prided marksmanship, sturdiness, ability to drink booze and, later, hatred of Spain, as the most respected attributes a man could possess. These people spoke French, smelled of smoked meat and dung, and were basically content to live unbothered. That was until the Spanish grew aware of the unofficial colony in the northwest corner of Hispaniola—trading illegally with passing ships, speaking French and being altogether un-Spanish. After this, the Spanish hunted the *boucaniers*, who suffered repeated attacks aimed at wiping them out completely.

But the *boucaniers* were not going anywhere. They became expert boatmen, designing swift canoes and small single-masted vessels, which were used in incredible raids against Spanish ships. Their basic strategy involved swarming their prey in shallow water, moving in close and fast while riddling the Spanish crew with deadly

accurate musket fire and drawing up close enough
to jam the enemy's rudder before proceeding to
scramble up the stern and swarm the ship.

Under pressure from the Spanish, the *boucaniers*
were eventually pushed off Hispaniola to the
island of Tortuga. The years saw more and more of
them making the short migration, so that by 1630,
the small rocky island with the excellent natural
harbor became their headquarters. Within about
20 years, a Huguenot privateer named Jean le Vas-
seur appointed himself Tortuga's first governor
and built a heavily armed fort on a rocky promon-
tory that overlooked the entrance into the harbor.
Thereafter, it was infamously known as a pirates'
headquarters, a hive of degenerate murderers and
robbers who hunted the waters of the Caribbean.
Privateers were the main source of income; they
brought a share of their booty to the governor in
exchange for safe harbor, while making the local
tavern keepers and prostitutes rich with their
vices. After England's occupation of Jamaica in
1655, Jamaica's capital, Port Royal, entered direct
competition with Tortuga in doling out letters of
marque and collecting the resulting share of buccaneer booty.

In this competition, Henry Morgan was Port
Royal's favorite son—the champion of Jamaican
piracy, whose immense and inhuman raids would
propel him to a dubious eminence in his adopted
island home. He distinguished himself as one of

the island's premier fighting men in his early adventures, spending the years following the establishment of British Jamaica plundering Spanish settlements wherever he could find them. In 1662 and 1663, he captained ships of his own in two successful expeditions led by Admiral Christopher Myngs, plundering the settlements of Santiago de Cuba and Campeche. Months later, he was personally leading raids on Villahermosa and Gran Granada. His most famous exploit in the early years of his career was in 1665, when, along with the famous Dutch privateer, Edward Mansvelt, Morgan attacked and captured—for a brief time—the islands of Santa Catalina and New Providence.

Morgan would later say of his early years: "I left school too young to be a great proficient in that or other laws, and have been more used to the pike than the book." His was an education by way of experience, and he showed such exceptional talent in his apprenticeship of shot, sail, cutlass and cruelty, that he emerged in 1665 as a sort of living legend—a vicious fighter, an overzealous drinker, a leader among men. And he was only getting started. Whatever followed in the course of his life, Morgan was at his finest when carrying out seaborne atrocities against Spanish targets. Three historically brutal raids, conducted over a span of four years, would largely define his career: Porto Bello in 1668, Maracaibo in 1669 and the most famous of all, the sacking of Panama in 1671.

Porto Bello had become Spain's main treasure port on the Isthmus of Darien in the years following Francis Drake's 1572 raid on the Spanish treasure port. A much more established settlement in 1668 than Nombre de Dios had ever been, Porto Bello was considered one of the best fortified cities in the Spanish West Indies, boasting two well-manned forts that stood over the entrance of the bay, protecting the harbor and town. In addition to the reputed 300 soldiers stationed in the treasure port, there were roughly 400 families residing there, along with the seasonal merchants that came and went with the silver caravans from Panama. Porto Bello also contained two churches, a hospital and over 150 homes built solely for the traders and bureaucrats who managed the movement of silver. A real bid at permanent settlement, Porto Bello was a far cry from the unfortunate cluster of shacks on the water that made up Nombre de Dios.

Early in 1668, Morgan learned that the garrison at Porto Bello had been lessened, and he wasted no time in putting together a raiding party. In the early summer of that year, Morgan and more than 500 of the worst buccaneers he was able to find packed into 12 little ships and sailed forth with the blessings of the governor of Jamaica behind them. In the early evening of July 10, the party reached the Darien coast, casting anchor in the Bay of Boca del Tora, about four leagues west of Porto Bello. Five hundred men clambered down from the ships into 23 canoes, leaving behind just enough men to form skeleton crews in the sailing vessels.

Morgan knew the coast well and led his flotilla of canoes through the darkness. They rowed without word or whisper, beaching their canoes at Estera Long Lemos sometime past midnight. They carried their boats into the jungle and covered them with palm fronds. Then, tucking cutlasses into their belts, knives into their boots and shouldering their muskets, they continued on foot.

The first Spaniards they encountered were stationed in a lookout post on the edge of sleeping Porto Bello. There were a mere five guards watching the inland approach into town, and the buccaneers, approaching in darkness under the cover of the jungle's nocturnal chirp and whistle, took them completely by surprise. It was not until Henry Morgan emerged from the darkness to announce himself that the Spaniards grew wise to the danger.

Morgan knew five men against 500 was a quick fight, but intent on achieving surprise in Porto Bello, it was a fight he preferred to avoid. Torch in hand, the buccaneer chief strode before the small redoubt. The flickering fire in his hand cast red and orange light over the wide brim of his hat and the ferocious glare beneath. "Allow me, lads, to make it clear. Ye be looking at Henry Morgan, devil of these waters, marauder and murderer and mortal enemy to every Spaniard bastard west of

the line. I would sooner see yer fathers disemboweled and yer mothers sold to slavery than grant ye
a kind word," Morgan paused, spit at the ground
and shifted his gun belt.

"The 500 bastards what stand behind me be little better. Hell's coming to visit Porto Bello this
night, of that there's little doubt. Yet Lady Luck is
smiling at ye dogs, for there're few what fight
under Spanish colors this eve who'll be granted
what I'm about to offer. Put up yer weapons, come
down quietly and no harm will come to ye. Other-
wise, it's no quarter."

The men atop the makeshift fort were either too
brave or too incredulous to take Morgan's proposal
seriously and responded to the offer with a volley
of musket fire. One of the plumes on Morgan's hat
was shot off; another musket ball lodged itself in
his torch, but the guards' trembling guns did no
other damage to the bold buccaneer standing on
the trail. There was distinct joy in Morgan's face as
he roared, "Shoot these scurvy dogs dead!" Then
there was the sound of 100 muskets, the splinter
and tear of the wooden ramparts, the tumbling
death of the five Spaniards. Torch men ran up and
set the lookout post aflame. Porto Bello woke to
the sound of muskets and the fiery glow of the
burning redoubt on the edge of town. The raid had
begun.

Morgan had lost the element of surprise, but not
by much. Pulling a pistol from the sash around his

waist, he slashed his cutlass through the air. A terrible shout went up from the throats of 500 men, and they swept into the city. Morgan had told the truth. Hell came to Porto Bello. Confusion and panic swept through the city. Soldiers and militia grabbed their weapons and rallied in the streets, where they fell back behind the walls of their forts. Without any walls to flee to, the townsfolk were left to their own devices. There were those who thought of their wealth first, frantically dumping their valuables into wells and cisterns. Some, fearing for their lives in the face of Morgan's howling horde, ran frantically into the cover of the surrounding hills, while others stayed put, barring their doors, putting out their lights and praying for deliverance.

The buccaneers split into two parties. The larger group headed for the forts looking over the harbor; the other, on Morgan's order, made its way to the cloisters to fetch the priests, monks and nuns. A bloody tint was just beginning to spread over the early morning sky when Morgan and his men came up to the base of Santiago Castle, the largest of the three forts. They knew that the town gentry would be in Santiago Castle—along with their wealth.

There was another castle, the partly completed fort of San Geronimo. A far less imposing structure than Santiago, it presented a tempting target, and a small group broke off Morgan's force and rushed the fortification. Built on a small island just

off Porto Bello's quay, its best defense was its location. Yet the soldiers there surrendered without
firing a shot, the fight scared out of them by the
sight of the heavily armed buccaneers wading out
through the water.

The garrison at Santiago was not so easily cowed.
Morgan himself led the first charge against its
walls, but there the pirate attack was checked,
running into stiff cannon and musket fire that cut
deeply into its ranks. The number of corpses
mounted quickly as Morgan and his men returned
fire. The French musketeers in the pirates' ranks,
famous for their marksmanship, lived up to their
reputation, coolly dropping to a knee and picking
off any man on the ramparts who remained sta-
tionary for any length of time.

Yet the buccaneer's position was untenable.
Standing exposed beneath the walls, they were
being effectively butchered by the men above. They
would need scaling ladders to breach the walls, but
Morgan knew they could not hope to provide suf-
ficient cover for attackers hauling ladders.

A group of raiders rushed Santiago with hand
grenades. Morgan watched as half of the men were
cut down before they made it to the walls. Those
men still standing hurled their lit missiles at the
castle. Scattered explosions were followed by
plumes of smoke, after which the ramparts came
to life with musket fire, and a good half of the gre-
nade throwers were cut down.

"The devil!" Morgan shouted over the din. "Fall back, you lecherous vermin! Away from these walls!" It was not drum roll discipline that moved them, but self-preservation; never was a battlefield order so expeditiously obeyed. The buccaneers fell back in no good order, hollering curses as they went, some stopping to expose their privates to their enemies on the castle walls.

Henry Morgan stood in terrible silence amid his routed men, his eyes launching fiery ordinance at the castle in the distance. When a cheer went up from the Spaniards on those walls, he was seething. "Sink me!" he roared. "Who do these wretches think they're facing?" The buccaneers, who were likewise hurling oaths at the castle, fell silent. They all held their captain in such high regard that they were certain his fury alone could bring down Santiago's walls.

Morgan was pacing now, muttering unholy litanies, his imagination racing through a number of bloody strategies until it settled on one of the worst. "Lucifer's ghost!" he shouted. "Bring me their friars from the churches. Bring me their most revered priests and whatever nuns ply their holy trade in this poxed town!" There was a moment when Morgan might as well have been surrounded by statues, so still were the buccaneers, wondering if they had heard their captain's order correctly. "Drag out some of their women while you're at it," he added.

"You heard the captain!" came the shout from one of Morgan's officers. "Earn your pay, you lot! Comb the town and bring them out!"

The statues sprung to life. Urging one another on, they ran back into the city, flooding into the homes and pulling mothers from husbands and children. They also went to where the other party had secured the churches. Morgan's order was repeated, and not another moment was wasted. They dragged Porto Bello's most revered citizens—its priests, monks and nuns—out to the battle-field.

Within the hour, the wretched elect were lined up before the still-pacing Morgan, who appraised them with a vicious eye. "My, my, what a sight is this," he said, his scowl breaking into a hideous grin.

One of the priests stepped forward. He took a deep breath, drew himself up and looked Morgan straight in the face. "What do you want, dread pirate? Whatever abominable cause has impelled you to bring us here, know that we have no place in your battle. The men of the cloth and our sisters do not belong on this field. Leave the mothers be. Let the fight be decided among those who fight it."

Morgan nodded, as though in agreement, and then pulled a pistol from his waist, pressed it against the priest's forehead and, to a wailing chorus of protest, shot the man between the eyes. "That's a right decent notion, now, ain't it?" Morgan said to the very dead prelate, whose surprised eyes stared back. "The problem, however, is that decency doesn't concern me too much, 'specially when it comes to Spaniards."

He turned, then, to the rest of the assembled clergy and gave the incredible order. They were to take the scaling ladders, carry them across the open ground and place them against the walls of Santiago Castle. And lest they get any smart ideas, he told them, they would be marching out at the head of a mob of pirates who would not think twice about shooting them dead should they do anything but take the ladders forward. Did any of them not go out, then, with the scaling ladders on their shoulders, believing that their countrymen would not dream of opening fire on them.

Porto Bello's governor had been on the walls when the first shots were fired. He was still there, the most fervent fighter among them, urging his men to keep up the fire, all the while wielding muskets to considerable effect himself. Tireless, and courageous, the governor was a soldier by profession and a fierce patriot; he was determined to hold his post against this rabble that had lurched from the jungle—or die trying.

Appraising the advancing force before him, he hesitated only for a moment before issuing his order. "Fire on them. Those ladders must not reach these walls." A cry was heard, then, from a group of monks with a ladder that made up one of the front ranks. These monks called out to the men in the castle, imploring them not to fire but to surrender the fort and so preserve their souls.

The governor was the first man to fire, taking careful aim at a woman and pulling the trigger. His target cried out and fell but was immediately replaced by a friar, who, at the tip of a cutlass, took the woman's place. And so it began.

The musket fire was hesitant at first but picked up as the ladders drew nearer. Soon cannons joined the small arms, raining shot and cannonballs over the terrible massacre below. But despite the horrendous cost, the ladders went up, and as soon as they fell against the walls, the buccaneers were on them, dashing up with incredible speed, holding their knives in their teeth and their muskets in their hands. They swarmed over the castle like ants over tropical refuse. And yet somehow, the badly outnumbered Spanish managed to throw them back. They fought possessed on the ramparts, clubbing their attackers with the stocks of their muskets, cutting savage arcs with their blades. They fought desperately, like the cornered animals they were, and the buccaneers faltered, turned and retreated.

This time, there were no cheers coming from Santiago's walls, and when Morgan's men attacked again, it was with redoubled ferocity. They came at the castle in two groups, one with grenades and torches setting the gate afire, the second with ladders, clambering over the walls. The two-pronged attack proved too much for the defenders, and they surrendered all at once, throwing down their arms and pleading for mercy.

All except the governor, whose determination to fight had gone from valor to suicide. He ran through the castle, slaying surrendering Spaniards with the same vehemence that he struck at the attacking pirates. That was until his battle frenzy deposited him in a narrow doorway, facing off against a cordon of rather impressed buccaneers. The rough men found themselves moved by the governor's homicidal belligerence and offered him quarter.

"Better to die an honorable soldier than hanged as a coward!" came his shrill reply. They rushed him with the stocks of their muskets and the flats of their cutlasses, intending to take him alive. He put up such a fight that they had no choice but to kill him. Thus the assault on Santiago Castle was over the same day it began, its governor shot to death, its garrison captured and the wealthiest citizens of Porto Bello in the hands of pirates. One fort remained under Spanish control, the Castle of San Phillipe, across the harbor. But Morgan, standing atop Santiago's walls, was content with what his men had accomplished that day, and it was with a broad grin that he shouted the order from the ramparts: "Fall into Porto Bello, lads! Enjoy what she has to offer!"

Plunderers in the wake of victory have written some of history's darkest pages. The buccaneers led the prisoners from Santiago into the town of Porto Bello. They quartered the men in one part of town, the women in another, and then began to make the settlement into a debauched hellhole, drinking themselves beyond reason and brutalizing the inhabitants at their leisure. They helped themselves to the larders; they strung up and tortured the wealthy until they revealed where they had stashed their loot. Those who had nothing to reveal were whipped, beaten and dismembered before succumbing to death. There, on the edge of the jungle, Porto Bello raged with the fires of atrocity, where men fed by drink and madness committed acts unmentionable in these pages. They paused the next day, just long enough for Morgan to gather a battalion of 200 relatively sober men to capture the sole remaining fort on the harbor and allow his ships to join in the festivities.

When there was nothing left to restrain the buccaneers from their vicious appetites, they continued to inflict them on Porto Bello, staying on for three weeks, turning the Spanish town into a festering site of carnage and sin. Morgan's men were oblivious in their revelry, and wounded buccaneers and Spaniards alike died of neglect, while the piles of tortured corpses grew daily along with an ungodly stench that hung over the treasure port.

All the while, a joyous and debauched Morgan was in negations with the stunned viceroy of Panama, who could not believe that a band of buccaneers had managed to overrun the treasure port. From the safety of Panama, he demanded that Morgan and his forces withdraw, threatening them with the might of the Spanish garrison if they did not get back on their ships and leave immediately. But Morgan, not intimidated in the least, was quick to issue threats of his own, promising to burn Porto Bello to the ground if he did not receive 350,000 pieces of eight from the Spanish authority. The president of Panama's response was, "I take you to be a corsair, and I reply that the vassals of the King of Spain do not make treaties with inferior persons."

And so Morgan turned to Porto Bello's residents, threatening to put their homes to the torch if they failed to come up with a gesture of appreciation. After squeezing out a ransom of 100,000 pieces of eight from the horrified townsfolk, he loaded his men and booty onto his ships and left at his own leisure. Before he left, however, he sent the Panamanian viceroy one of the French muskets that had brought down the defenses at Santiago—a gift, he said, which he would return to claim in the next year or two. If the viceroy of Panama scoffed at Morgan's audacity, he knew nothing of the ambition that boiled within the buccaneer chieftain.

Morgan and his men returned to Jamaica as heroes, their holds bursting with Spanish treasure, which they promptly spent in fine piratical fashion, cavorting for weeks without restraint in the streets of Port Royal. The Spanish Ambassador in London made noises that Porto Bello had been attacked weeks after Spain and England had signed a peace treaty, but King Charles was not at all chagrined at the zealousness of his subjects, and Sir Thomas Modyford, the governor of Jamaica, received neither admonishment nor any order to return Porto Bello's booty.

While Modyford was enjoying a period of impunity under the British Crown, it was not long before Henry Morgan began to feel the pressures of his station. Buccaneers were hardly known for any kind of financial prudence; it was not long before the spoils of Porto Bello had run out, and Jamaica was bristling with restless seamen eager for another job. Morgan's ultimate goal was wealth and respectability, but his heart was with the cutlass-bearing swabs he drank and fought alongside. In October of 1668, mere months after returning from Porto Bello, Morgan made it known among the buccaneers that he was planning another raid.

He sailed out to Isla Vaca, off the southwest coast of Hispaniola, where he established a temporary base. Morgan did not have to wait long before ships flying under black banners began to arrive. There were Frenchmen from Tortuga, English privateers from all over the West Indies, Dutchmen, former slaves, ambitious adventurers and anyone else hoping to become rich at the expense of the Spanish. By January the next year, there were 10 ships and over 800 men gathered in his camp.

Despite this impressive response, Morgan's second major Caribbean campaign did not have the most auspicious start. One of the mightiest ships in Morgan's fleet was the HMS *Oxford*, a 34-gun warship from the Royal Navy that had been commissioned to defend the waters off Jamaica. Something between patriotism and love of violence swelled in Morgan when he caught sight of the *Oxford* weighing anchor at his Isla Vaca headquarters. He promptly made the *Oxford* his flagship and called his commanders together to discuss the coming campaign—a raid on the treasure port of Cartagena. The commanders arrived onboard with their bodyguards, and while Morgan and his senior officers were discussing strategy in the poop deck cabin, the bodyguards were celebrating in an exceedingly piratical fashion, awash in prodigious quantities of rum, grog, wine…and gunpowder.

The commanders in the poop deck hardly noticed when the revelers began discharging their muskets, certainly a healthy way for swabs to demonstrate their appreciation of a good party. But when the celebration moved on to the gun deck, with ceremonial cannon fire that caused the whole ship to shake, Morgan might have decided that the cavorters had gone too far. If, at that point, he thought about reigning in the festivities, he never had the opportunity to give the order. A moment later, a deafening roar emerged from the *Oxford's* belly, followed by a fiery explosion that tore through the center of the ship, ripping from hull to deck and rending the ship in two.

The immediate aftermath saw between 200 and 300 men floating lifeless amid the flaming wreckage of the once-powerful *Oxford*. Twenty or so men were still alive, thrashing in the water among the dead. Incredibly, Morgan was among the survivors, somehow thrown clear of the roaring conflagration that claimed almost everyone else on board.

No one knew for sure what had caused the blast. Suspicious minds pointed to the tensions between the English and French among Morgan's men. They insinuated that some bitter Frenchman angry about a past disagreement over misappropriated booty had set the gunpowder in the magazine on fire. Those who wanted to keep the French sailors among them discounted this theory. Morgan himself had no desire to lose any more men and quickly put the matter to rest by insisting that the explosion had been an accident, set off by a drunken reveler whose musket fuse had fallen too near a powder barrel.

The loss of the flagship and over 200 souls was a massive blow to Morgan's ambitions. Still, he was determined to stage an operation against the Spanish colonies. The well-fortified Cartagena was no longer a possibility for his diminished force, so Morgan decided on an alternate target: the lightly defended towns and forts dotting the Venezuelan coast around the enormous lagoon of Maracaibo.

Morgan's fleet set sail for Venezuelan shores, where they enjoyed over a month of practically uncontested raiding among the settlements within the Maracaibo lagoon, taking what they wanted, torturing slaves and colonizers alike and cavorting at their leisure. Beyond livestock, some modest wealth and the settlers' dignity, there was little to plunder on the coast. Indeed, it was a rather undistinguished operation, which would have likely been forgotten all together if not for its dramatic conclusion.

The Maracaibo campaign became a much more urgent affair upon the arrival of Don Alonzo de Compos y Espinosa, Admiral of the Spanish fleet in the West Indies, intent on stopping Morgan's depredations. The Admiral appeared at the mouth of the lagoon with three massive warships, bristling with enough cannons and mariners to pulverize Morgan's force three times over. Occupying the fort at the mouth of the lagoon, Espinosa took control of the sole exit, thus trapping Morgan and his men in the vast lake.

The message the Admiral sent to Henry Morgan survives as one of the most famous documents from the piratical era in the West Indies:

Having, through our friends and neighbors, received news that you have had the audacity to commit hostilities in the territories and cities owing obedience to His Catholic Majesty, the King of Spain, my master, I have come to this place, according to my bounden duty, and have built up again the fortress which you took from a set of faint-hearts and from which you flung down guns, that I may prevent your escape from this lake and do you all the injury my duty requires.

Nevertheless, if you will surrender with humility all which you have taken, including the slaves and other prisoners, I will have the clemency to let you pass, that you may return to your own country. Should you obdurately resist these honorable conditions which I propose, I shall send for sloops from Caracas, in which I shall embark my troops to sail for Maracaibo, with orders to destroy you utterly and put every man to the sword. This is my final resolution: take heed, and be not ungrateful for my kindness. I have with me valiant soldiers, yearning to be allowed to revenge the unrighteous acts you have committed against the Spanish nation in America.

Signed on board His Majesty's ship, Magdalena, at anchor in the entry of the Lake of Maracaibo, 24 April 1669.

–Don Alonzo del Campo y Espinosa

THE THREE CAMPAIGNS OF HENRY MORGAN

In one of the great displays of the democratic spirit that prevailed in the pirate hierarchy, Morgan gathered his men in the Maracaibo marketplace and had Espinosa's declaration read, in both English and French. He informed them also of Espinosa's strength and position before putting forth the question, "What would you have me say to this man's proposal?"

The response came from a hundred throats at once, a fierce acclamation that made it clear that there was not one among them who had any intention of parting with a single ounce of their spoils. Morgan lifted his own voice to join the roaring defiance. "So be it, brethren!" he called out over the vicious congregation. "We will give this Don Alonzo a show he shan't soon forget!"

He sent back his reply—he and his men would leave Maracaibo untouched if they were allowed passage from the lagoon unmolested with their possessions intact. When the admiral promptly responded that his demands were not up for negotiation, Morgan immediately set to work. The Spanish warships were the first matter of business.

Knowing full well that he did not have the firepower to stand against Don Alonzo's fleet, Morgan devised a plan to create the illusion of firepower. He ordered a recently captured Cuban merchant ship to be disguised as an imposing warship, with extra rows of gun ports cut into the hull and logs stuck into them to look like cannons. On the deck, more trunks were placed along the gunwales and painted to look as though the ship was manned by a full contingent of sailors and mariners. In reality, there would be nothing more than a skeleton crew piloting the vessel, 12 men whose orders were to sail it right up to the Spanish flagship before lighting a coiling network of fuses and making their escape. The idea was to get away before the lit fuses made their way below deck to the ship's payload, a hold packed to capacity with barrels of gunpowder. Was Morgan inspired by his experience just a few months previous at Isla Vaca? The force with which the *Oxford* went up must certainly have been on Morgan's mind when he envisioned the damage a ship loaded with explosions could inflict.

On April 30, with Henry Morgan's flag flying high on the dummy ship's mainmast, the buccaneer fleet arrayed itself behind the converted Cuban vessel and sailed out to meet Don Alonzo. They came upon the Spanish fleet anchored at the mouth of the lagoon. Under supporting fire from the vessels behind, the merchant ship headed straight for Alonzo's flagship, the 412-ton *Magdalena*. The 12 buccaneers piloted the explosive-laden vessel right up to the massive Spanish galleon, lighting the fuses once they had fastened their vessel to the flagship with grappling hooks. Only after the 12 men were rowing safely away did the sailors on the *Magdalena* realize that there was no boarding party set to sweep aboard their ship. Only then did they look through the mist of gun smoke to see that the men on board the Cuban vessel were actually dressed up logs, and that only a very small number of the cannons jutting from the gun ports were real cannons. Frantic orders to detach the grappling ropes sounded up and down the deck, but the fuses had already reached the merchant ship's lower decks. The ensuing explosion instantly incinerated Morgan's decoy. Flames rained upon the *Magdalena*, which promptly caught fire and floundered as the Spaniards who survived the initial blast dove headlong into the surrounding waters.

Don Alonzo was one of the survivors. Pulled to the safety of one of his subordinate's ships as the buccaneers withdrew from the battle, the Spanish admiral's arrogance hardened into burning rage. When Morgan attempted to renegotiate his passage, Don Alonzo refused to consider anything besides complete surrender. While the admiral's squadron had definitely suffered a crippling loss in the sinking of the *Magdalena*, the Spanish were still in control of the fort that looked over the lagoon entrance. The fort was manned by a full garrison and armed with heavy artillery placements, more than enough to pulverize any vessels attempting to run Don Alonzo's blockade.

Knowing full well that he did not stand a chance in a straight fight, Morgan once again went for the feint. As dusk fell, Morgan emptied his ships, sending all his boats ashore, crammed with heavily armed buccaneers. The move was made in plain sight of the Spanish fort. Convinced that Morgan was getting ready for a land attack, Don Alonzo ordered all his artillery be moved to cover the buccaneers' landward approach. When the landing boats appeared again from the cover of the coast, the Spaniards saw they were all but empty, save for the handful of men who were rowing them back to where Morgan's fleet was anchored. In fact, not one of the buccaneers had disembarked. Once the boats had beached, the buccaneers had fallen silent and lay flat under the thwarts, so that they were effectively hidden as the boats returned to the ships.

Thus Alonzo and the Spanish garrison kept their eyes and guns trained on the surrounding jungle, completely unaware of the fact that every buccaneer was back aboard his ship. In the absolute darkness of the small hours, Morgan whispered the order to weigh anchor and ride the tide past the Spanish blockade. Don Alonzo's men were so certain a small army teemed in the darkness of the jungle that they did not notice Morgan's vessels slip by. Not until it was too late. Morning's first light revealed the buccaneer fleet out in open water, well out of range of the Spaniards' heaviest guns. The faint sound of whistles and jeers carrying across the water would remain with Don Alonzo for the rest of his days.

Morgan and his flotilla of buccaneers returned to Port Royal as victors once again. While the Maracaibo raids were not nearly as lucrative as the sacking of Porto Bello, in terms of glory among the rough denizens of Port Royal and Tortuga, the tale of the buccaneers' escape was worth a fortune. Word of Morgan's triumph over the humiliated Don Alonzo made its boisterous way through the seaside taverns of the Caribbean. If there had been any doubt of the Jamaican privateer's laurels, no enemy of Spain thought of questioning them anymore.

While the engagement did much to burnish Morgan's reputation among his fellow buccaneers, the English Crown was less than pleased. Sir Modyford was informed that the official peace between Spain and England could no longer permit the unofficial hostilities in the West Indies to continue. While London was willing to let the plunder of Porto Bello go, Modyford was informed that he was not to issue any more letters of marque to ambitious buccaneers.

The order would be a blow to English privateers based out of Port Royal, who would gravitate to Tortuga for the necessary paperwork to "legally" raid Spanish ships. Modyford was not thrilled either, as the Jamaican treasury lost no small amount of revenue from the loss of its share of privateer booty. Henry Morgan, however, welcomed the reprieve. He made the rounds of the Port Royal taverns, where he was greeted as a hero, drank excessively and spun gruesome stories of his adventures. He also expanded his holdings on the island, buying 836 acres that would come to be known as Morgan's Valley. Also, it is said, he spent some time with his wife.

And yet events would conspire against any sort of lasting peace. For even as Modyford received the order to cease raids against the Spanish, the Queen of Spain sent the governor of Cartagena a letter ordering him to begin distributing letters of marque against the English. Too long had the Spanish suffered relentless piracy; it was about time they employed some privateers of their own.

So it was that an ambitious Portuguese corsair named Captain Rivero unleashed a series of attacks against British holdings in the West Indies. He first emerged in a series of raids on the Cayman Islands; next, he was sighted off the coast of Cuba, where he attacked a Jamaican privateer. Then, in June of 1670, he attacked Jamaica itself, landing a raiding party in Montego Bay and ravaging a settlement. Soon after that he was on the south coast, raiding another coastal settlement and putting the torch to two buildings.

Captain Rivero's operation was modest by Morgan's standards, but it was more than enough to prompt the Council of Jamaica to act. The colony's statesmen met and quickly arrived at a decision— revenge. They decided that "a commission be granted to Admiral Henry Morgan to be Admiral and Commander in Chief of all ships of war belonging to this harbor," which he was to use "to attack, seize and destroy all the enemy's vessels that shall come within his reach," as well as invade any Spanish lands he saw fit.

On August 1, 1670, just over a year after Maracaibo, Morgan received his commission to visit destruction upon the Spanish. It was the closest Morgan would get to an official call to arms—a clear order to retaliate against an enemy that had attacked the colony. Despite the previous order from England, Governor Modyford drafted up a letter of marque for Morgan, granted him a flagship and sent him on his way.

It may have resembled an official call to arms, yet Morgan still recruited from the pool of men he had such affinity for—the lowest caste of seamen in the West Indies, the loathed and feared buccaneers. Word quickly spread through every tavern from Port Royal to Tortuga: Henry Morgan was launching another campaign. He was mustering men and ships at Isla Vaca. Two months later, Morgan was presiding over the largest fleet he would ever command; there were 38 ships moored off the small island, with over 2000 depraved souls waiting to do his nefarious bidding. With such a force, Morgan's ambitions reached for one of the greatest Spanish cities in the West Indies.

Panama (today's Panama City) was the most important treasure port on the Pacific Coast. With a population of roughly 6000, it served as the hub of all the gold and silver from Peru and the mines of Bolivian Potosi. Thus Panama was very well fortified. Its president, Don Juan Pérez de Guzmán, made sure of it, ensuring the city was well stocked with armaments and manned by a strong garrison consisting of nearly 2000 foot soldiers and a contingent of 400 cavalrymen. There was a general belief that no standing army in the West Indies could hope to mount an assault on the bustling colonial city.

But a motley gathering of English, French and Dutch buccaneers did not really qualify as an army, and Morgan himself was certainly no army commander. His scope and understanding of violence went far beyond the typical military convention that defined the officer class of that time. And he was willing to gamble everything to satisfy his immense ambitions.

It was late December 1670 when Morgan's fleet descended upon the north coast of the Isthmus of Darien. The first difficulty they encountered was the castle of San Lorenzo, situated at the mouth of the river Chagres. Planning to take the Chagres as far toward Panama as they were able, they could not pass before silencing the guns of San Lorenzo. This proved to be far more difficult than Morgan had ever imagined.

Indeed, the planned assault on Panama came very close to being turned back before it had even begun. Beginning at day's last light and continuing throughout the night, Morgan's buccaneers repeatedly threw themselves at San Lorenzo's walls, only to be turned back time and again by the castle's stubborn defenders. The pirates worked themselves into a screaming, homicidal frenzy. They roared curses at the Spanish civilization and rushed forward with ladders, muskets, grenades and cutlasses. Over and over again, they were repelled by musket fire and heavy ordnance from the ramparts above. But in the end, fortune picked the side with the longer list of sins. The morning's early light brought heavy wind, and a spark from a fire inside the fort was carried onto a hut's roof. The dried palm thatch caught fire and spread quickly.

While the Spanish were busy containing the fire, the buccaneers struck again, breaking through the fortifications and into the chaos that reigned within. Once the pirates were inside, the Spanish resolve dissolved like lime in brine. The reason they had put up such a fight in the first place was because each man knew what horrors buccaneers visited on their prisoners. Wholesale suicide ensued as Spanish soldiers hurled themselves from the castle walls rather than be captured by Morgan's murderous mob. There was neither pause nor remorse after the battle. The buccaneers stopped just long enough to hoist the red and white of St. George's Cross over the castle before moving on.

They took the ships as far up the Chagres as they could go. The order was given to drop anchor, and the men began unloading canoes. Filling the heavy green waters, the 100 canoes were packed with 1200 men. The rest were left behind to guard the ships. The ugly cavalcade pulled up at Cruz de San Juan Gallego, where the water was too shallow to continue. Another 160 men were separated from the main force with orders to watch over the canoes. Cinching their bandanas tighter around their heads, and strapping on their pistols, muskets, cutlasses and daggers, the buccaneers said farewell to their comrades and plunged into the sweltering jungle.

If they had known what was waiting for them, they might have chosen to burden themselves a little less with weaponry in favor of more food. Assuming that they would be able to make their way by foraging and pillaging food as they came across it, the buccaneers soon discovered that the Spaniards had learned of their arrival and had taken great pains to ensure their 10-day trek to Panama would not be a pleasant one.

They were able to deal with the grueling march, the sultry heat of the jungle, the swarms of insects and the occasional Spanish ambush, but the starvation they suffered along the way tested the limits of their endurance. Anticipating Morgan's march to Panama, the Spanish left vast swaths of scorched earth where their maize fields had been. For meat, the buccaneers found reeking piles of rotting cattle. The Spanish destroyed whatever they could not take with them. Morgan's zealous crew of 1200 was reduced to a ragged, half-starved band staggering through the jungle. Delirious with hunger and beset by tropical fevers, many men became too weak to continue. With each passing day, Morgan lost ever-increasing numbers to hunger, disease and desertion, so that by the time he emerged from the wilderness onto the plain before Panama 10 days later, he had only 800 men with him.

And these were not typical fighting men. The 800 men who made it through the hellish trek were vibrating with homicidal energy. Carrying with them the madness of hunger, the horror of the jungle and the memory of their dead comrades, the buccaneers who arrayed for battle behind Morgan on January 28, 1671, were nothing less than the distillation of their brutish caste. Stripped of whatever vintages of temperance and civilization they may have still carried, they greeted the promise of battle with a terrifying enthusiasm, screeching and rattling their cutlasses as they fell into line. There, in front of them, were the spires of Panama at last, finally within reach. The fact that there was an army that outnumbered them more than two to one standing between the buccaneers and their goal did nothing to dampen their battle lust.

For the nearly 2000 men standing with Don Juan in front of Panama, it must have seemed as though the worst of hell's demons had come out of

the jungle that morning, so vicious did the emaci-
ated and mud-caked maniacs appear. And yet
there were also such a piteously small number of
them; for all their ferocity, the pirates were still
outnumbered. The Spanish took comfort in their
own numbers, especially the 400 horsemen
seated imposingly in their saddles. What chance
did the insane rabble of buccaneers have against
400 charging cavalrymen?

They would soon find out. Morgan, seeing stra-
tegic advantage in occupying a hill on his enemy's
right flank, ordered one of his squadrons to veer
off and take the high ground. The Spanish interpreted the move as the beginning of a general
retreat, and the 400 horsemen rushed forward.
After what they had been through, the buccaneers
did not so much as flinch as the earth trembled
under the hooves of their enemies.

"Muskets!" Morgan shouted. But the French
skirmishers at the fore of his men had already
begun firing—the best shots in his troop picking
off the horsemen with deadly accuracy. Before he
could see what was happening to his cavalry, Don
Juan urged the main body of his men forward,
and on they went with a deafening shout. Confidence quickly melted into confusion as the Spanish cavalry, cowed by the withering musket fire
from the French sharpshooters, came galloping
back through their comrades' ranks.

Morgan saw his opportunity. "Advance and empty your muskets!" came the order. "Into their ranks! The dogs!" The buccaneers advanced several paces before opening up. The confused mass in the center of the plain quickly became a roiling, bloody mess of terrified soldiers who fell into a disorganized rout.

Don Juan still had his trump—two enormous herds of some 2000 oxen that he intended to send stampeding across the battlefield. He envisioned a wave of horns and hooves razing the pirates from the ground. What was about to transpire was far less impressive. On his order, the *vaqueros* managed to send the beasts galloping toward Morgan's lines, but the lumbering approach of these creatures had the opposite effect of what was intended.

"Sink me!" one buccaneer shouted. "They tried to starve us, and now they're sending us fresh meat!" Perhaps Don Juan did not realize the effect a herd of cattle would have on a horde of starving men. The buccaneers did not balk, but practically rushed forward, so eager were Morgan's men to get at the stringy animals. Thus the stampede faltered as well, and the oxen fell in among the confused mess of foot soldiers and horsemen.

Less than two hours after it began, the battle in front of Panama was over, as the buccaneers charged all at once into what was left of the defenders, throwing aside their muskets to hack at the fleeing Spaniards' backs with knives, pikes and cutlasses. Don Juan's defeat could not have been any more absolute. He lost roughly 500 men on the plain to Morgan's 15.

And the bloodletting had just begun. Over the next three hours, the buccaneers took the fight into the city, battling building to building against their panic-stricken enemy, destroying everything in their path. Pandemonium reigned as townspeople fell alongside soldiers. While the battle against the soldiers was carried on by a number of the buccaneers, some of Morgan's men began to celebrate—plundering, torturing and drinking. Dead cattle were hauled off the battlefield and cooked over the flames of burning buildings.

Fire consumed all of Panama that day and into the night; by the next morning, the once lofty colonial city was relegated to rubble and ash. The cathedral's tower and a scattering of other stone buildings were the only structures still standing. Scorched ruins and wailing residents—this was the prize Morgan and his men wrested from the authority of Don Juan. The destruction of Panama would go down as the grandest, ugliest piratical feat of the age. And yet there is some disagreement as to who was responsible for lighting the fires beneath the city.

One version of the history places the act on the shoulders of Don Juan. Having removed the bulk of the city's riches and vacated its elites on ships before Morgan's raiding party arrived, the admiral also rigged the city with powder kegs and fuses in case he lost the battle in front of the city. Or so the story goes. When the buccaneers stormed into Panama, Don Juan ordered the firing of the town, and thus the fires swept through the city. In the other version, the buccaneers, victorious against a larger army after starving for 10 days in the jungle, lost themselves in an orgy of violence. Swept up in the insanity, Morgan himself gave the order to spare nothing, to set the whole city to the torch.

Either way, Panama was destroyed. The Spanish who had survived the conflagration were doomed to reside in what was left of the city with the attackers for over a month. There, they were subjected to unspeakable madness, suffering every means of torture and degradation. Flayed, cut open, burnt alive, stretched, dismembered—the beastly buccaneers were remorseless in their interrogations, always to the same end: "Where be the gold? Where be the silver? Where be the jewels, ye Spanish bastards?"

In the end, these questions would never be answered to the pirates' satisfaction. For even when they extracted all the treasure they could manage, setting back to their canoes with no less than 175 mules packed full of precious booty and 600 prisoners for ransom; even after they made it back to their ships without losing a single saddle-bag and sailed back to Port Royal, where word of the sacking of their incredible accomplishment had already begun to spread—after everything they had been through, the buccaneers received no more than 200 pieces of eight per man. The sacking of Panama was indisputably the greatest pirate raid to date, and yet the sturdier among them would be able to burn through their share of the booty in about a month of frequenting taverns and bordellos. So the legacy of Morgan's greatest operation amounted to shiploads of bitterly incredulous buccaneers, angry and suspicious that their commander was making away with far more than his fair share.

But that was as far as it went. Such was Henry Morgan's reputation among the buccaneers of his day that not one among the hundreds of discontent seamen dared to act on his resentment. Most of the Frenchmen headed back to Tortuga and Hispaniola, while others set sail for the Bay of Campeche and Honduras. The rest followed their captain to Port Royal.

Escaping the animosity of his men, Morgan was greeted as a hero upon his arrival in Jamaica. Sir Modyford was more than pleased with the blow Morgan had dealt to the Spaniards. When the governor and Council of Jamaica met on June 10, 1671, they issued a public statement of gratitude to Morgan for executing his commission so effectively. "I think we are pretty well revenged for their burning our houses on the north and the side of this island," Sir Modyford's brother wrote after learning of the raid.

And yet a victory for the colony did not always amount to the same for the Crown in London. England and Spain were officially at peace, and while modest operations, such as Captain Rivero's 1670 raids on Jamaica, could be overlooked, a direct attack on a major city could easily be interpreted as a declaration of war. The destruction of Panama was a major blow to Spanish interests in the New World, and the Queen in Madrid was beside herself with rage. Having no desire to be cast into open warfare with Spain, the English Crown wasted no time reminding Modyford that he had breached the limits of his authority in assigning Morgan's commission.

Thus the British defused the situation by casting the responsibility on an irresponsible Jamaican statesman. Sir Thomas Lynch was sent overseas to replace Modyford as governor, arriving with secret orders to have Modyford arrested and sent back to London. There, Modyford would spend two years imprisoned in the Tower of London. Still, the Spanish were not placated, and in April 1672, Henry Morgan himself was arrested and sent back across the Atlantic.

For nearly two years, Morgan awaited judgment for his illegal attack on Panama, but none ever came. Instead, he spend his time in London rubbing shoulders with an enthralled English elite, spinning tales of his Caribbean adventures. He was knighted by Charles II and made such an impact on the English upper crust that he was asked to draft and submit a report to the King on how to improve Jamaica's defenses.

Meanwhile, Governor Lynch was having a tough time in the West Indies. Increasingly worried that the French were going to attack Jamaica, he was sending a fearful deluge of reports to London about his island's imminent attack. It was his persistent cries of wolf that convinced the authorities he might be lacking the mettle to be governor of the colony. In January of 1674, Lynch was informed that he was going to be replaced by Lord Vaughan and that Sir Henry—the man he had arrested— was now a knight and was to be appointed as Vaughan's lieutenant-governor.

Morgan returned to Jamaica in an official capacity as a confirmed member of the ruling class. Lieutenant-governor was an illustrious title, but as it turned out, not one that fit Morgan so well. He had been a buccaneer for too long; the conventions and restraints in "proper society" did not come naturally. Certainly Governor Vaughan did not appreciate the fact that his lieutenant was so undignified in his bearing. More than once, the governor grumbled about Morgan's "imprudence and unfitness to have anything to do with civil government."

There was no denying that Morgan spent more time swilling rum in Port Royal's seaside taverns than he did in councils of government. He was a stubborn, swaggering, hard-drinking lout, more suited to battle and plunder than backroom politicking. Yet somehow, he outlasted Vaughan in colonial politics, assuming the role of governor when London sent a missive relieving Vaughan of his duty. Thus Morgan became Jamaica's provisional leader while the island was waiting on the next appointment.

His short period of rule was rather unexceptional, marked only by Morgan's shoring up of the island's defenses as a response to reports of a looming French fleet. But no attack came, and Morgan restrained himself from launching any attacks of his own. Not that he was in any shape to command men in battle. The years of peace had not been kind to Morgan. Years of zealous consumption of food and drink did not go well with the sedentary life of a gentleman.

He was only 40 years old in 1687, when the next governor, the Duke of Albemarle, dropped anchor in Port Royal, but there was much of the grave in Morgan's appearance. Chronically ill for months, he was suffering the effects of severe edema, with a belly swelling through the confines of his greatcoat, a hacking cough and labored breath. Colony physicians had been urging him to rest, but Morgan refused to refrain from his dissolute lifestyle, continuing to imbibe mass amounts of alcohol as his heath deteriorated.

Morgan eventually gave up on his doctors and their repeated calls for temperance. He went to the black healers, medicine men who employed mysterious African treatments. He was stripped and covered in water and clay and subjected to a urine enema, but this was no more effective than any remedy the European physicians prescribed.

Henry Morgan died on August 25, 1688. Word spread quickly from his plantation estate. As soon as the Duke of Albemarle heard, he ordered a state funeral for the ex-pirate. Henry Morgan may have been a buccaneer and a lout who made his name by murder, torture and theft, but he was also Jamaica's champion in a violent and uncertain time. Laid in state at the King's House in Port Royal, Morgan was carried to his final resting place amid ceremonial cannon fire—a sailor and a buccaneer buried with the highest honors.

CHAPTER THREE

The Savage Rise and Dismal Fall of François L'Ollonais

FRANÇOIS L'OLLONAIS HAD BEEN A ship's captain for two years, maybe three, when he sailed into the storm that sank him. As with so many of the events in this infamous pirate's short and brutal life, the dates are uncertain. It is generally accepted that he started sailing Caribbean waters in 1660, and that he had only just begun to earn his grisly reputation when the tropical squall blowing across the Gulf of Mexico blindsided him and his crew. Sometime between 1662 and 1663, then, a modest, single-mast ship was being swept across churning waters off the coast of Campeche—beneath the relentless downpour of a heavy, thundering sky.

If he was as adept at sailing as he was at violence, L'Ollonais might have had better luck piloting his vessel through this storm. But his rigging was slack and tangled in the water, his mainsail was dangling like a flag in the wind and his keel was practically skidding sideways into the swells as foaming water poured over the bulwarks. Barely holding on with his helmsman next to the wildly spinning wheel, L'Ollonais could not think of a single order he might give in the face of such chaos. He and his men were at the mercy of the sea. The coastline was in sight when the ship finally floundered and sank.

Clinging to barrels and ship fragments in the briny toss, L'Ollonais' crew managed to kick their way through the violent waters to the safety of shore. Incredibly, not a man was lost. Each of the pirates was accounted for, soaked through and gasping for breath on the Yucatan beach. And yet before any of the robbers could think of thanking the Almighty for the miracle of their deliverance, the worst of their troubles quickly descended.

Spanish voices sounded in the distance, followed by the staccato crack of a round of musket fire. A shower of lead balls made thumping noises as they landed in the wet sand around the men. "Soldiers!" shouted one of the pirates. And there they were, a contingent of Spanish men on the beach, running toward the pirates, their steel breastplates a dull gray under the cloudy sky. There were too many, armed with muskets, pistols, swords and pikes. L'Ollonais and his men dragged themselves to their feet and ran, stumbling exhausted in the sand. Perhaps it would have been better if the sea had taken them.

The Spanish in Campeche knew there was a new menace stalking their waters. Many small merchant vessels had been boarded and relieved of their cargo in previous days. Survivors spoke of a French pirate captain with vicious eyes and a perpetual sneer, who called himself L'Ollonais and was fond of inflicting appalling atrocities on captured crewmen. Needless to say, Spanish soldiers and sailors on patrol were not inclined to be overly gracious to any unidentified crewmen in the area. Having spied the sinking pirate ship from shore, the Spanish were certain they had identified their quarry. They did not bother challenging before opening fire.

Running across the wide-open beach, most of the pirates were cut down before they made it to the cover of the tree line. L'Ollonais himself was grazed when a round of fire cut down several pirates around him. After losing his footing, he did not get back up but crawled on his belly to a dead man who lay nearby, covered in blood. Still lying flat, L'Ollonais dug his hand into the dead man's musket wounds and spread the man's blood over his own arms. Working quickly, he dug deeper into the wound and used the blood to cover his coat. He then poured a handful of sand over his face, obscuring the exhausted flush on his cheeks.

Having finished his disguise, L'Ollonais lay still, playing dead as the soldiers rushed by. A few of the Spaniards stopped quickly to finish off the wounded, but the pirate captain made such a convincing corpse that they did not look at him twice and continued on, following the other soldiers into the trees. There was a moment of quiet before the trees came to life with the sound of musket fire and clashing steel. L'Ollonais finally moved, scampering in a running crouch away from the fighting.

Thus the pirate captain had made his escape, but now he was alone and deep in enemy territory, the only nearby settlement he knew of being the Spanish city of Campeche. Binding his wound and burying his weapons, L'Ollonais set out for the city, practicing his Spanish to himself as he went. The streets in Campeche were full of his enemies; if he were found out, he would face the twine and gallows. But the town was the only place where he could secure escape, where there was a harbor with ships bound for all ports. Or, it should be said, not *all* ports. Indeed, there was no ship in Campeche that would willingly take him to lawless Tortuga, his intended destination.

A thought struck him soon after he arrived, while he was standing on the waterfront, watching a group of slaves unloading goods from a merchant ship. *Of course—there is no shortage of black pirates in Tortuga, practically all of them escaped slaves.* Slaves in Campeche would not fear the renegade island that he was destined for. Indeed, many of them may have dreamed of it. Authority relegated the slaves to their hated status, so would not rebellion against this authority amount to a step toward freedom? These men, L'Ollonais knew, would help him get back to open water. But he would have to be careful.

The pirate captain took his time, gradually getting to know the men on the docks over the course of several days while keeping up his guise as a traveling Spaniard. In that time, he witnessed first-hand the extent to which he and his kind were reviled in the Spanish ports. Word of the attack on him and his men got out quickly and was greeted with general celebration. A few of L'Ollonais pirates had surrendered to the soldiers. Dragged into the dungeons of Campeche, they were repeatedly pressed for the whereabouts of their captain. With implements of torture nearby, these men all gave the same answer as quickly as they were able. "He is dead!" It was the response they knew the Spaniards wanted to hear, and for all they knew it was the truth.

On the streets, L'Ollonais watched as the entire city celebrated the news of his demise. They drank, sang and burned effigies of him outside of taverns. Public prayers were held in the town center, where the kneeling residents gave thanks to God for ridding them of such a despised and cruel pirate. Having been at piracy for just a couple of years, L'Ollonais must have been at least a little surprised by how well known he already was—surprised, and, without doubt, more than a little bit pleased.

Still, the popular enthusiasm over his death could not have made him feel too at home, and he did not waste much time approaching the dockyard slaves he had been watching. The arrangement was simple—if they helped him abscond with a seaworthy vessel so he could escape to open water, he would guarantee them their freedom when they disembarked.

"And where we be headed?" one of the men asked.

L'Ollonais cast a careful look over the docks before replying. "Tortuga," he whispered. The light that came on in the slaves' eyes was proof enough to the pirate that his idea about these men had been correct. "Yes, my friends, you shall be pirates if you want it, living free as kings off the spoils of these blighted Spaniards." He paused, making sure there was no mistake about his next point. "*If* you help me escape."

When the slaves returned that night, they came with what little possessions they owned. Their courage was up and they burned with dreams of emancipation. L'Ollonais met them in the darkness, his grin visible in the silvery light of the half-moon. "So then, maties," he whispered, "what say we heave ho?"

A few weeks later, they piloted a cramped little sloop into the pirate haven of Tortuga—the slaves now free men and L'Ollonais eager to get back to sea. News of the disaster of his last expedition had spread quickly, and the pirate had some difficulty getting another crew together, but it was not long before L'Ollonais was back out on the water, aboard a leaky vessel with a small crew of ruthless seafarers under his command.

This time he did not go far, trolling Cuba's southern coast near the village of De los Cayos. L'Ollonais now had a deep, burning hatred, a profound need for vengeance against the Spanish. His crewmen saw the terse urgency of this need in their captain as he paced the decks, but none could guess at the depths to which it ran—at the simmering violence that was about to boil over into infamy.

Villagers of De los Cayos precipitated the coming battle when they spied L'Ollonais' approaching vessel, boldly sailing under a fluttering red flag— the color of no quarter. A messenger was immediately sent to the governor in Havana—the townspeople were in need of aid; pirates were in their waters. The governor, a man who had an especially foul opinion of the area's seaborne robbers, gave the word for a ship to be sent out to meet them. The Spanish ship was a stout 10-gun vessel manned by 90 fighting sailors and one hangman, who was added to ship's crew by the governor himself. The crew's orders were simple—do not return until the reported vermin in our water be removed, and hang them all from the mast of their ship, excepting their captain, who you will bring back to Havana alive.

By torturing a number of fishermen, L'Ollonais learned of the approaching vessel. Mooring in a partly concealed cove, he transferred his men into canoes stolen from the fishing village. They waited.

When the Spanish arrived, they moored off De los Cayos, where they were promptly attacked. L'Ollonais and his men came at them early in the morning, when the waters were still and the sun was low. They attacked in the fashion of the first buccaneers, paddling hard in long canoes and pulling up on both sides of the ship, then clambering up the hull with their weapons in their teeth and setting upon their quarry with cutlass, knife and pistol. Taken unawares and shocked by the zealousness of the pirates' attack, the Spanish put up a ferocious but short-lived fight before surrendering to the mercy of their assailants. They would soon learn that there was no mercy, no good grace, not even a dram of kindness in L'Ollonais heart.

After first commanding that the prisoners be locked under the hatches, L'Ollonais had them brought up one by one, where, each man in his turn had his head hacked from his neck by L'Ollonais' blunted cutlass. Some of the men were asked questions: "What is yer purpose in these waters?" or "Who sent ye?" or else "Are ye a Spaniard native born?" Others faced no query but were only treated to a disdainful sneer before their necks were severed.

The hangman's turn came. He was prodded from below deck, pale and trembling at the sight of the massacre. "I know a swab when I see one," the well-sated L'Ollonais said, wiping the blood of his latest victim from his blade. "And I can see clear as water that ye be not."

The man managed to shake his head.

L'Ollonais let out a clipped guffaw and looked gleefully at his men. "Let this be a lesson to ye lot. Same as the devil, I can see the soul of a man."

He turned his attention back to the hangman. "So then, matey, what be your purpose on this fair ship?"

While L'Ollonais spoke, the captive was gaping horrorstruck at the human heads piled against the gunwale. He turned to the pirate captain. "I was the hangman."

"A hangman!" L'Ollonais said. "Ahoy! This be a great honor! A live in-the-blood Jack Ketch! Tell me, matey, be it in the Spanish tradition to carry gallows men aboard their vessels?"

The hangman was still reeling in mute shock, not thinking as he muttered his response. "The governor put me aboard. Execute the crew—all but the captain. Bring back the captain."

Gasps and strangled laughter carried over the deck. "Did ye hear that swabs?" L'Ollonais hollered. "This man was to be yer executioner, while I was to enjoy the governor's table!" When he turned back to the hangman, there was no trace of the mockery that had been there before; a cruel fire now burned in his eyes. "Well, friend, I'll have ye know that isn't the way of the buccaneers. We drink and dine together." A cheer went up from his men, and L'Ollonais swung his weapon, decapitating the hangman in two ugly blows.

And it continued—bodies in one corner, heads in another, the deck awash in blood. The captives pleaded, they fought, they finagled—but L'Ollonais was unmoved and dispensed his summary executions until there was but one Spaniard left. This man's life was spared.

"I have a message for your master," L'Ollonais said to the last crewman. "Go back to Havana. Tell the governor what you have seen here today. Tell him one man did this. That man is myself, the pirate François L'Ollonais. They were sure I was shark bait in Campeche, but I sail these waters yet and will continue until the devil takes me back. Until then, tell your governor in Havana this— I shall never henceforth give quarter to any Spaniard; and I have great hopes I shall execute on him the very same punishment I have done upon them he sent against me. Thus I have returned the kindness he designed for me and my companions."

The governor of Havana received the message from the traumatized sailor, and the first page of the legend of François L'Ollonais was written in the blood-soaked annals of piratical history. He was called the cruelest buccaneer to ever sail Caribbean waters, the "Flail of the Spaniards," the most perverse and psychotic captain who ever hoisted the flag of no quarter, killing not only for money, but because he took no small degree of pleasure in snuffing out the life of Spaniards. François L'Ollonais was as bad as it got.

And yet as infamous as he became, very little is known of L'Ollonais' origins. It is said his real name was Jean-David Nau, and that he was born around 1835 in a region in France called the Sables d'Ollone, hence his namesake. Histories that say anything about his provenance in the West Indies place him as an indentured servant arriving on the island of Martinique at around 1650. After roughly 10 years of labor, he managed to save enough to buy his freedom. Drifting across the West Indies, he stumbled upon the buccaneer settlements in Hispaniola and Tortuga. His early adventures as a Caribbean freebooter won him something of a reputation among his almost exclusively Spanish targets, but it was not until his declaration to the governor of Havana, when L'Ollonais rose from the dead to personally decapitate an entire crew, that his bloody star was born.

After sending his message to the governor of Cuba, L'Ollonais returned to Tortuga to plan his next expedition. About 500 men emerged from the inns and taverns to answer his call, rootless degenerates to a man, eager for booty and violence. In April of that year—placed anywhere from 1663 to 1666—L'Ollonais set sail for Maracaibo at the head of his small fleet.

From the outset, fortune was smiling upon the wicked flotilla. Spotting a Spanish ship near the eastern cape of Hispaniola, L'Ollonais himself led the assault, shouting nefarious vows over roaring cannon and musket fire. After grappling hooks were lodged into the gunwales of the Spanish ship, L'Ollonais was first onboard the enemy deck. Two hours later, it was he who took the Spanish flag down from the mainmast and gave the order for every prisoner to be executed and thrown overboard. And he got richer for it. The Spanish ship was carrying thousands of pounds cacao, about 40,000 pieces of eight and a fortune in jewels.

The party continued south for Maracaibo amid much celebration. They apprehended one more ship, which was likewise boarded and ravaged, before reaching their destination. By the time they reached the Gulf of Venezuela, they were drunk beyond reason on rum and invulnerability. They were unstoppable, this howling mob of bloodthirsty seamen—and they were ready to descend on the settlements along the Maracaibo lagoon.

The first was the city of Maracaibo itself. Along with a population of approximately 4000 Spanish colonists and African slaves, there was a garrison of 800 soldiers and militia. This was well over the number of men sailing with L'Ollonais, and the Spanish enjoyed the advantage of defense as well—but any comparison on numbers alone fails to account for the zeal and homicidal fury of the sons of Tortuga. By all rights, the men of Maracaibo should have fed the buccaneers to the sharks, but the devil himself was riding on L'Ollonais' shoulder.

The campaign began with an attack on the fort guarding the entrance into the Gulf. L'Ollonais had his fleet drop anchor well out of sight of the fort walls, then led the pirates on a march across land. Their attempt at stealth was unsuccessful, however, and the Spanish set up an ambush in their path. L'Ollonais and his men fought through it, viciously and fast, killing every man in their path. Barely pausing to bury their dead before soldiering on, the buccaneers arrived at the castle that same day and defeated the overwhelmed garrison in just three hours. Routed and demoralized, the surviving soldiers fled into the city of Maracaibo, where they sounded the alarm. Church bells rang over the general panic as the news went from house to house—thieving murderers numbering in the hundreds had broken through into the lagoon and were heading toward the city. And at their head was the demon himself—François L'Ollonais.

The pirates came seething into Maracaibo a few short hours later, covered by the guns of their ships, but the city had already been abandoned. Men, women and children, soldiers, merchants, farmers and slaves, had all fled, taking with them what possessions they were able, streaming into the surrounding woods or taking any available vessel to the town of Gibraltar on the other side of the lagoon.

Thus there was very little of value for the pirates to plunder, but they made the most of the situation, availing themselves of the huge stores of fine tobacco, fresh victuals, rum and cacao. They ransacked administration buildings and homes alike, scouring every space for treasures that may have been left behind. And they paid their respects to Maracaibo's residents by making themselves at home—sleeping in their beds after falling besotted from drinking their rum; massacring their livestock; reaping their harvest; and extending their stay in the city for as long as there were free provisions to be had.

In the 15 days that they stayed there, L'Ollonais' men also managed to get some work done. Establishing a headquarters in the central church, they collected the townspeople within its stone walls. L'Ollonais ordered search parties be sent out into the surrounding jungle on the trail of the escaped. They brought back far too many.

Colonists living in the jungle were retrieved, bound and beaten, along with whatever possessions they had taken with them. The first foray alone yielded over 20 prisoners as well as mules packed with valuables and roughly 20,000 pieces of eight. Most of the prisoners were tortured to force an admission of additional treasure buried in the jungle. Most of them had nothing to confess and were tortured to death on racks over open flames, under the sharpened knives of their tormentors.

Two weeks later, after L'Ollonais' men had stripped Maracaibo of everything they could, the pirate captain set his craven eyes across the shallow waters of the lagoon. There, roughly 100 miles to the south, lay Gibraltar. It was a smaller settlement than Maracaibo, but L'Ollonais knew its numbers would have swelled with the arrival of Maracaibo's refugees. He also knew that many of these refugees were likely the city's richest, who had taken their valuables with them. Certainly, there would be generous booty to be had. And if not, at the very least there would be more Spaniards to torment.

The Spanish, however, had other ideas. L'Ollonais was correct in thinking that Maracaibo's wealthiest had fled to Gibraltar ahead of the pirates, taking their treasure with them. Most of these colonists were not planning to stay put in Gibraltar, either, but were making ready to escape further inland to Mérida; until, that is, the governor of that city received news of the invasion. A military man who had served in European battles, Mérida's governor was hardly intimidated by L'Ollonais' pirates. He sent a message to Gibraltar, instructing residents and refugees alike to say put. They need not come to him; he would go to them and bring with him 400 fighting men, effectively doubling the town's standing garrison.

So it was that when L'Ollonais' fleet approached Gibraltar, they came upon a town that was ready to fight, with the Spanish colors flying high over fortified positions and a garrison of 800 soldiers. The sight of the reinforced batteries facing the water was imposing enough to cause the dreaded buccaneer to balk. Dropping anchor out of cannon range, L'Ollonais held a council of war, presenting the situation as best as he was able.

"Gibraltar is girded for a fight and will not easily fall," he said. "Their batteries cover the water, and I'll wager my helmsman's right arm the landward approach is the same. Nothing is sure, but my blood tells me they have numbers and if we launch this attack, victory will not come easily." He paused and looked each man in the eye. "If we land, this will be a good brawl, and I need to know yer mettle is up to it."

An uneasy silence followed. The buccaneer code did not allow for fear in the face of the enemy, especially if that enemy was a Spaniard. The floor was open, but no man was ready to express anything that approximated doubt. "It don't matter if all of Spain be waiting in Gibraltar," one man finally spoke. "The devil's sailed with us into this here lagoon, and there's not a dog on this ship what doubts it. So let's quit dawdling and have at these Spaniards."

Shouts went up across the deck as every pirate gave his lusty assent. "Very well then," L'Ollonais said. "We must go to battle like good soldiers or lose our lives with all the riches we have got. Do as

I shall do, who am yer captain. The more of them there are, the more glory we shall attribute to our fortune, and the greater the riches for the taking."

A chorus of oaths sounded through the ship. Each man swore to do his duty—which was generally a pledge buccaneers liked to avoid. After the buzz of self-congratulation settled, however, L'Ollonais added his final thought on the matter. "'Tis well, ye make a most fortunate captain out of me," he said with a grim smile at the general show of loyalty, "but now that it's decided, know ye withal that the first man who shall show any fear or the least apprehension thereof, I will pistol him with my own hands."

Thus it was resolved to begin the assault the next day at first light. The waters were calm when they dropped anchor, about a mile from town and the pirates rowed ashore. However, their march to Gibraltar was soon cut short. A barricade had been erected in their path, in the middle of open ground, manned by many soldiers and too many cannons to make passage by that route feasible. Taking another approach, they soon found themselves hacking through heavy jungle.

The battle for Gibraltar began here, while the men were cutting their way forward. By making their own path, the pirates avoided a costly frontal assault on a barricade, but they were still well within firing distance of the Spanish defensive positions. As soon as they learned the pirates were slashing a path to Gibraltar, the Spanish opened fire on the disturbance in the bush. The barrage of cannon and musket fire made a tremendous racket, sending a tremor of panic through the buccaneers' ranks.

But they quickly learned the bombardment was not as bad as it sounded. L'Ollonais and his men were well concealed within the trees. While the Spanish had a general idea of where the pirates were, they could not effectively concentrate their fire. The fact that a thick cloud of gunpowder smoke soon covered the area did little to help the Spanish cause. Through it all the pirates came. Through the smoke, the sustained whine of musket balls and the rumble of cannons they continued to slash away at the bush, holding on by force of will and a promise of booty. A number of them fell, hit by the haphazard gunfire, yet the spectacle of the Spanish defense was far more impressive than it was effective. After the alarm of the opening shots, the buccaneers steeled themselves and pressed forward.

However, their hard resolve was about to waver. Coming out of the jungle onto the open ground before Gibraltar, the buccaneers stood in front of another strong fortification. Six cannons filled with grapeshot immediately opened up on them, followed by a withering round of musket fire from over 200 guns. Bodies fell at the edge of the jungle, and the pirates stopped, suddenly cowed by the realities of their assault. Now that they were standing in front of the town, the idea of rushing at the well-positioned Spanish bore too close a resemblance to suicide.

Those who had not already headed for the cover of the jungle absorbed another barrage from the Spanish and then stood for a moment longer as a huge shout sounded from the barricade, followed by hundreds of sword-wielding soldiers rushing out toward them. No order to retreat was necessary. The pirates plunged back into the jungle, a terrified mob falling over one another to get as far away as they could as quickly as they were able. The soldiers quit the chase before they were too far into the trees, and L'Ollonais was soon able to rally his men.

Crowded together in the cover of the trees, the buccaneers pulled themselves together and reorganized for another attempt on the town. Moving out with the hopes of finding another approach, they soon discovered that the Spanish had constructed a meticulous defense. The buccaneers had already fled from the only viable approach. And hours after their first aborted attack, this was where they returned.

This time, L'Ollonais had a plan. It was a desperate tactic, and after hearing it a good number of his men would have reconsidered the vow they had taken. But whether it was confidence in his leadership or fear of his pistols, the men fell in line at the edge of the trees, readying themselves for a frontal assault. The pirate captain gave a shout, and they charged out from the jungle and onto open ground. They ran headlong, brandishing cutlasses and pistols, screaming wildly as muzzles flashed and cannons erupted from the fort. Many of them fell, and those who made it to the fort barricades had no way of gaining entrance under the pressure of the Spaniards' point-blank fire.

Only lasting several minutes so close to their enemy, the pirates turned and ran in a disorganized rush back to the treeline, looking every bit the defeated army. A cheer rose from the fort, along with spontaneous orders to pursue the fleeing band. The soldiers came running from the cover of the barricade. They charged out in a confused mass, certain of their victory over the buccaneers, not suspecting for a moment that the attack and hasty retreat they had witnessed was nothing more than a ploy to draw them out of their fort.

In the cover of the jungle, L'Ollonais and his men took up positions concealed in pre-ordained ambush sites, quietly waiting for their brash enemies to arrive. The Spanish were caught completely by surprise, meeting a determined and coordinated counterattack among the dense foliage. With pistol and cutlass, the buccaneers cut into their bewildered opponents. Most of the Spanish fell dead in the opening moments of the ferocious ambush; the rest were sent reeling back to the safety of their barricade. Few made it back alive, a good number of them being cut down in open view of villagers and soldiers in Gibraltar.

To those Spanish who witnessed the previously victorious soldiers now running pell-mell back for the safety of the fort, it must have seemed as though the devil was indeed fighting with the pirates. For the buccaneers came out of the jungle on the heels of the last Spaniard, howling in victory with bloodied weapons in their hands, taking remorseless vengeance as they swept into the now unmanned fort. The spectacle was enough to instantly kill the Spanish will to fight. Resigning themselves to defeat, the soldiers in the other barricades gave up their arms on the condition that the pirates would grant them quarter. The citizens in Gibraltar, suddenly at the mercy of the pirates, fell into general disorder, some fleeing into the surrounding woods with what they could carry, others putting themselves at the mercy of the occupiers. But L'Ollonais' pirates came with sword, fire and pandemonium, and there was little mercy to be had.

The first thing they concerned themselves with was keeping the town. Fortifying the town's church, the pirates took defensive positions around Gibraltar's center. They gathered the 500 Spanish dead who had fallen in the battle and put them onto two ships moored in front of the town, sending them into the lagoon and then sinking them when they were about a mile offshore. They buried the 50 or so of their own dead in shallow graves at the edge of town. Their wounded, who amounted to about the number of dead, were put into several houses designated as hospitals. Over the course of the occupation, most of these men died of fever, infection and neglect.

After a few days, when it became clear that the Spanish had no intention of mounting any sort of counterattack, the buccaneers sank into the iniquitous rituals of piratical plunder. They gathered all the townsfolk who had been foolish enough to remain. They pillaged their houses. They tortured, raped and killed. They uncovered hidden treasure based on information they extracted from their prisoners. They went out into the surrounding wilderness to hunt down those who had fled.

L'Ollonais' band remained in Gibraltar for no less than four weeks, consuming Spanish provisions while those Spanish prisoners not subject to lethal torture or random execution slowly starved to death. The buccaneers unearthed more treasure each day, even as a pestilent cloud of death and decay grew thick and heavy in the tropical heat. The pirates left only after they had reduced Gibraltar to a smoldering husk, stripped of everything that had even the smallest value. Not only its gold, silver and jewels, but also its steel, weapons, rum and hides. Their avaricious eyes missed nothing; their depravity knew no bounds.

There was still the final affront. They sent several prisoners who had managed to evade capture by the Spaniards and were hiding in the surrounding hills. Their message: come up with 10,000 pieces of eight in two days or else what's left of Gibraltar will be burned to the ground. When two days passed without a response, L'Ollonais gave the command to set Gibraltar to the torch. Half the town was incinerated before its inhabitants managed to come up with the ransom. Incredibly, the buccaneers helped the surviving inhabitants put out the rest of the fires before departing.

Harassing the city of Maracaibo for more loot on their way out to the Caribbean, L'Ollonais' band took another 20,000 pieces of eight and the meat of 500 head of cattle. Their ships bloated with treasure, the fleet sailed to the northern coast of Hispaniola, where they moored their vessels and divided the loot. It was a whale of a take, with treasure amounting to some 260,000 pieces of eight to be divided among L'Ollonais' crew.

From Hispaniola it was a short journey back to Tortuga. Gone for just over two months, the pirates returned with full pockets and grand tales involving the death and degradation of countless Spanish. By buccaneer standards, the expedition was a brilliant achievement. The men who carried it out were envied in every inn and tavern, and the captain who led them through it became a revered celebrity. After his adventures in the Maracaibo lagoon, François L'Ollonais was propelled into the piratical pantheon, where he would remain ever after, despite his next horrific voyage that was to be his last.

Because of the success in Maracaibo, L'Ollonais had no problems recruiting men for his next adventure. Pirates came crowding to his banner, so that he soon was in command of no less than 700 men divided into six ships. This time the heading was west toward the Cuban shoreline and beyond. It did not take long for things to start going wrong.

After robbing a settlement of tortoise fishers in Cuba, the fleet lost its way in the Gulf of Honduras and was waylaid in still waters that saw them eat through almost all of their provisions as they sat stranded. When they finally reached coastal waters, they fell upon native settlements that had very little in the way of riches—a fact which did little to deter the pirates from murder and plunder. Entire villages were wiped out for their stores of millet, hogs and hens.

And things did not get much better. Waiting for more favorable sailing weather, the band went aimlessly up and down the coast, hitting several humble settlements, finding just enough in the way of provisions to keep the quickly souring expedition going. When L'Ollonais and his men came upon Puerto Cavallo, there was reason to believe their luck had finally changed. Here, perhaps, there would be some booty for the restless buccaneers.

The small Spanish settlement was not marked on any of their maps, but it looked promising enough, with a good-sized ship docked at its harbor, two sizeable storehouses on the waterfront and a relatively large cluster of houses. It was not much of an achievement for them to overwhelm the small town's defenses, yet neither was there much booty to be taken. The ship's cargo had already been emptied, and the storehouses contained nothing of any value. L'Ollonais and his men took their frustrations out on Puerto Cavallo, burning it to the ground and killing all but two of the town's inhabitants.

From these two men, the buccaneers learned two things—merchant ships were due in port some time over the next few months, and there was another settlement called San Pedro a few days' march inland from where they were. So it was that L'Ollonais set out with 300 of his best men, leaving the rest behind to guard over Puerto Cavallo in case the merchant vessels arrived while they were gone.

The march to San Pedro did not go well. In the jungle, they suffered three separate ambushes by Spanish soldiers, who seemed to know the exact route they were taking. The pirates fought through each attack but not without paying a price. Their casualties mounting, the men made their way through the swelter as best they could. But the smallness of the plunder taken so far, combined with the strain of possible ambush in every bend in the trail, had their effect. The Spanish soldiers who survived the ambushes were subjected to the worst atrocities the buccaneers knew. It was during this trek that, while interrogating two captured soldiers about the possibility of another ambush, L'Ollonais cut the heart out of one prisoner and ate it right before the other soldier's eyes.

Thus while the pirates' morale was sinking, their zeal for murder and iniquity was still undiminished. The attack on San Pedro was vicious, a full day of relentless attack and brutality that ended at nightfall, with the inhabitants waving white flags of surrender. But the treasure the pirates hoped to find was not there. Just as in Puerto Cavallo, there was little in San Pedro worth stealing. Most of the town's inhabitants, having had warning well in advance, had fled before the buccaneers arrived. Taking the half-deserted streets as a personal insult, L'Ollonais and his men visited terrible retribution on the remaining townsfolk, before reducing the town to ash and rubble. They left the devastated San Pedro a few days later and marched back to Puerto Cavallo, where their companions were languishing.

Not a single merchant ship had docked there while L'Ollonais had been gone, and the men were beginning to run short on provisions. Still with next to nothing to show for their efforts, the fleet set sail for a cluster of nearby islands to search for food and a place to careen their hulls. They ended up spending the better part of three months drifting along the coastal waters, finding just enough provisions to keep the expedition going and nothing at all that resembled treasure.

For most of the sailors, this was their first raiding expedition against the Spanish. They were young inexperienced seamen, who, hearing of the massive wealth L'Ollonais plundered on his Maracaibo campaign, rushed into his service, assuming the same riches would come their way. None of them had guessed that the path to booty would take so long or be so arduous. And with each passing day, more and more of them began to question if there would be any booty at all.

Their faith finally crumbled when the long-awaited merchant ship appeared in the waters off Puerto Cavallo and was boarded and captured, only to yield a half-empty hold of metal plates and cacao beans. What aura of authority L'Ollonais had left evaporated onboard the Spanish vessel, and the merciless buccaneer found himself staring down the hard looks of hundreds of angry and exhausted men.

Sensing impending mutiny, he called a council on the poop deck of his ship, where he hoped to restore his men's waning confidence by proposing a new destination—the waters off Guatemala. But it was too late. A handful of leaders let it be known that L'Ollonais no longer had the loyalty of the men. The situation became dangerous on more than one of his ships.

The democratic process in the pirate hierarchy was one of the defining factors that set it apart from the rigid order of command that existed on naval and merchant vessels. While disobedience in the navy could see a man keelhauled, bowsprited or worse, pirate captains only retained their authority so long as their crew believed them to be the most capable to lead. It was not uncommon for a pirate captain to relinquish control to an able first mate who was popular with the crew.

Yet relinquishing control proved to be well beyond L'Ollonais capacity, and even as he was presented with the short and dismal history of the current expedition, he insisted that certain riches awaited those who continued to take his orders. In the end, he was only able to convince a small number of sailors that he was still fit for command. He retained his ship, while the rest of the buccaneers departed in all the others, under the command of a seaman by the name of Moses Vanclein, who decided it was time to call it quits and head back for Tortuga.

As it turned out, despite L'Ollonais' highest ambitions, things did not get any better for him or for those few who still called him captain. Indeed, things got incalculably worse. First beached in the Gulf of Honduras on account of shallow waters, he and his crew were forced to subsist on monkey meat and rainwater while waiting for favorable sailing conditions. Soon after they finally made their way out, they fell afoul of a sandbar off the Isle of Pertas.

With no hope of dislodging the ship, the sailors were forced to take the vessel apart and construct a longboat that would be able to traverse the shallow waters. During the arduous months of construction, the castaways lived off what they could find on the island, all the while managing to keep up a functioning chain of command. Somehow, L'Ollonais' authority persisted, despite the isolation and grueling labor. When the primitive craft was finally completed, he selected a crew to pilot the vessel to friendlier waters, promising the men he left behind that he would return for them as soon as possible. After waiting many months, these men resigned themselves to the fact that they would never see François L'Ollonais again and ended up joining the crew of a Jamaican pirate who happened to be passing by.

The castaways ended up faring much better than the sailors who were picked to accompany their cursed captain. Landing on the Honduras coast, L'Ollonais and his men were ambushed by a combined force of Spanish soldiers and native warriors. L'Ollonais and a handful of his buccaneers managed to escape, but not before a brief and vicious fight, which left half of his men dead or dying on a bloodstained beach.

For L'Ollonais and his followers, the end came on the Darien coast, where they were attacked by a party of native warriors. They were slaughtered to a man. L'Ollonais himself was reportedly torn limb from limb, cooked over a fire and eaten by gleeful and remorseless enemies—a fitting conclusion for one of the wickedest buccaneers who ever sailed the West Indies.

∾⋙✕⋘∾

PART TWO

The Golden Age of Piracy

IT DID NOT LAST LONG, this much-storied boom of plunder and mayhem concentrated in the Caribbean, the Gulf of Mexico and the Atlantic Coast of North America, but in the decade or so that it went on, an entire mythology was born. At the heart of pirate mythology was a dissolute pantheon of seafaring ne'er-do-wells who were more than thieves and murderers but were also stubborn individualists and violent libertarians, living in an age when such sensibilities made them outlaws. These were the men who became the raving anti-heroes most of us today recognize as the pirate stereotype—cruel, murderous, corrupt, but also admirable in their boldness, their refusal to conform to the mores of their day. For it was no small thing to go pirate, declaring one's self at odds and at war with the authorities.

This is just the mythology, however. The seminal work written on this generation of freebooters was Captain Charles Johnson's *A General History of the Robberies and Murders of the Most Notorious Pyrates*. Its first edition was published in 1724, in the midst of the piracy epidemic that seized the waters of the "New World." Johnson's book did not paint these men in flattering colors, but it was an immediate sensation. The idea of these rebellious, often piti-less robbers defying order and authority in the waters on the edge of the world was irresistible to the reading public.

Romanticism aside, piracy's golden age was actually born *of* royal authority, rather than in opposition to it. The problem with recruiting privateers to war against an empire's enemy was the glut of fighting sailors left without employment once the fighting stopped. Edmund Dunner, who pioneered the first mail service to the West Indies, stated his opinion on the practice of privateering: "...this cursed trade will breed so many pirates that, when peace comes, we shall be in more danger from them than we are now from the enemy." Dunner could not have been more prophetic. King William's War ended in 1697, and Caribbean ports, crowded with men who had been making a living raiding Spanish shipping, became recruiting places for piracy.

The phenomenon was repeated after the War of Spanish Succession was resolved in 1713. English privateers who had engaged in Crown-sanctioned seizures of French and Spanish shipping suddenly found themselves out of work. The frenzy of piracy that followed lasted well into the 1720s. It ground to a halt only after much effort on the part of the Royal Navy, which hanged a small army of pirates.

CHAPTER FOUR

The Dread Pirate Blackbeard

In the commonwealth of Pyrates, he who goes the greatest length of wickedness is looked up on with a kind of envy amongst them, as a person of more extraordinary gallantry, and is thereby entitled to be distinguished by some post.

—Captain Charles Johnson, 1724

IN THE LATE AFTERNOON OF November 21, 1718, Lieutenant Robert Maynard stood on the prow of his sloop, his spyglass trained across the shallow waters of North Carolina's Ocracoke Inlet. Two vessels. One was of no consequence—a small shipping craft or tender, bereft of all but a skeleton crew. The other was of far more interest. Armed heavily with cannons at the gun ports, its decks were strewn with some 25 to 30 sailors, singing, shouting and shooting muskets at the clear blue sky. Emptied and half-emptied bottles of rum rolled with the swells, back and forth over the deck.

The sight of such drunkenness on deck was a great offense to Lieutenant Maynard's military sensibilities. "Vermin," he muttered, wincing through his spyglass.

But there was much vermin in the seas of late, and it would not do to attack just any crew of

drunken sailors. He was after one in particular—
the ugliest and most dangerous, who had every
seafaring merchant from the Caribbean to the
North Atlantic considering alternatives to their
line of work. Maynard had been ordered into the
waters off the North Carolina coast to apprehend
Edward Teach, a.k.a., Blackbeard. Sent by Governor Spotswood of Virginia, Maynard had no official authority in the colony of North Carolina and
so had to be careful to apprehend the right ship
and get away as quickly as possible.

Slowly moving his telescope over the length of
the ship, the lieutenant jumped at what he saw
when he reached the stern. There, standing straight
at the gunwale, a man with a telescope was staring right back at him. Refocusing, Maynard looked
on as the man across the inlet put down his lens
and went storming across his deck. There was no
doubt: the veins bulging from the man's neck; the
roaring rage in his eyes; the coarse mass of black
hair, huge and unruly, sprouting from his cheek-
bones and hanging down to his chest; and the
ship's name, *Adventure*, scrawled across the stern.
Yes, there was no doubt. Maynard was looking
across the inlet at the greatest menace of the seas.

The lieutenant was too far away to hear what
Blackbeard was saying, but he clearly saw the
effect the pirate's orders had on the cavorting crew.
Men lying in a drunken stupor snapped to atten-
tion. Bottles were cast aside. Sailors took position.
In turn, Maynard spun to shout orders at his crew,

calling the 35 sailors and mariners on his ship to
battle stations. He also gave the signal to his consort, the 25-man *Ranger*, letting its commander,
midshipman Baker, know that they were staring
down the real thing. The two commanders from
Virginia would be expected to bring back the
pirate or embrace Davy Jones trying.

Neither side made a move. All ships anchored
and the crews spent the night making ready for
the inevitable battle—Maynard with his men putting together a strategy, Blackbeard with his men,
drinking up the remainder of their supply of rum
and celebrating late into the night. When morning
came and Maynard saw that his quarry had made
no move, he acted, sending out small boats to gauge
the water's depth between him and the *Adventure*.

Although Maynard made the first move, it was
Blackbeard who fired the opening shots. His cannons launched a screaming barrage at Maynard's
boats as soon as they were within range. None of
the boats were hit, but the cannonballs splashed
close enough to deter them from continuing. The
lieutenant watched his men row frantically back
to the sloop, resigning himself to the fact that he
would have to engage the enemy without any sure
knowledge of the lay of the water.

Because the *Ranger* had the shallower draft,
Maynard ordered Baker ahead to feel out the low
waters, piloting his own vessel close behind. They
had not made much progress toward Blackbeard's

Adventure when Maynard ran aground on a sand-bar that Baker had just cleared. Even as the lieu-tenant issued frantic orders to dump his ship's ballast overboard, Baker's sloop hit a sandbar as well and was likewise stopped dead in the water. So it was that Maynard floated out without his ballast and bore down on Blackbeard on his own. Baker's men were still emptying their water casks in hopes of rising in the shallow waters.

"Damn you for villains! Who are you? And from whence came you?"

The voice belonged to none other than Edward Teach. He was close enough now to be plainly seen—a tall man, over six feet, in a sun-bleached greatcoat and tricorne, his heavy beard plaited into thick tendrils tied with bright ribbons. Two lit fuses protruded from both sides of his hat, wreath-ing his head in black smoke. He had a bandoleer loaded with pistols over his shoulder, a cutlass in one hand and a bottle of rum in the other.

Maynard ordered the British ensign be raised. "You can see by our colors that we are no pirates," he shouted back.

There was an ugly grin and a wild look on the face of Edward Teach. "Colors surely be the cox-combry of the seas, matey. I invite you to come aboard me ship so I can get a better look at ye."

Maynard drew his cutlass. "'Tis a funny thing," he said. "Me and my lads were planning just such a visit, whether we be invited or no. I cannot spare my boat but will gladly come alongside as soon as I'm able with this sloop."

Blackbeard let out a hellacious guffaw before taking a last swig of rum and throwing the empty bottle into the salty water. "Blaggard! Damnation seize my soul if I give you quarter or take any from you!"

"So be it," Maynard shouted his reply. "No quarter asked. None given."

Even as Maynard turned to give the order to go full sail ahead, Teach had his Jolly Roger run up his topmast. It was his personal insignia, the horned Death's Head on the black flag, and it grinned down as the deck of the *Adventure* came to life. Teach barked commands between curses as sails were unfurled, the anchor cable was cut away and the cannons were loaded.

Rum-addled as they were, Blackbeard's sailors were able, and they knew the inlet well. It was no great thing for them to swing past Maynard's clumsy maneuvering and head for the open waters past the cove. By this time, Baker had finally managed to clear the *Ranger* of the sandbar and was moving to intercept the *Adventure*. Blackbeard did not adjust his course until he was close enough to throw a stone onto Baker's deck. It was then that he gave the order; sailors heaved on the rigging, the mainsail snapped taut, and the *Adventure* swung around to present her broadside to Baker and his suddenly terrified crew.

"Give 'em a whiff!" Blackbeard's shout was followed by the blast of cannons. Shot and cannonballs swept over the *Ranger's* deck, instantly killing Baker, his two top-ranking officers and several sailors, while shredding the foremast and the jib. Thomas Tucker, the master mate, picked himself up from among the dead and wounded, wasting not a moment before taking command of the crippled vessel. With no sails at the fore, the *Ranger* was beyond control and began drifting out of the fight. Still, Tucker did all he could, shouting at the surviving crewmen to come up to the gunwales with muskets and powder. In a matter of minutes, there was continuous small arms fire coming from the damaged deck of the *Ranger*. They succeeded in shooting out Blackbeard's front halyards and jib.

The wind died, then, and Maynard, striving to join the fight, called on his men to retrieve the oars. His deck was crowded with men pulling at the sweeps when they finally caught up to the *Adventure*. As they came, the pirates hove at their mainsail, turning tightly so that they were to present their broadside as Maynard fell into close range. Blackbeard saw that his enemy's deck was crowded with men at the sweeps and shouted for the cannons to be crammed with shot.

Then Teach gave the order and the *Adventure* unleashed her second broadside that morning, sending a shower of lead across Maynard's deck. Twenty-one of the sloop's 35 sailors fell wounded under the devastating barrage, and Maynard, fearing a complete massacre if Blackbeard should fire again, ordered every man still standing to run for cover below deck.

It was a ruinous barrage. When the smoke cleared, Blackbeard surveyed the carnage on the sloop before him and was convinced that his enemy had been defeated. He drew the *Adventure* up against the sloop as his men hurled makeshift grenades over the gunwales and fired their muskets at the deck. Through the black smoke curling up from Maynard's sloop, there was almost no visible movement. "There's nothing left o' them, me hearties!" Teach shouted. "All hands! No quarter! Board her and feed them to the fish!"

A shout went up from the *Adventure*. Teach and his men rushed over the gunwales. They boarded quickly, clambering onto the English sloop with the devil in their eyes, sure that they were there to mop up what was left of the pulverized crew. But a cruel surprise awaited the pirates. For, below deck, Maynard and his men were still alive and well. While the salvo of grenades and musket fire had made a fierce racket, there was not a single casualty among those mariners who had retreated with their lieutenant. In breathless anticipation, they waited for Maynard's word, packed close in the darkness beneath the deck, cutlasses drawn, pistols and muskets loaded.

The lieutenant did not give the order until he was sure all the pirates were onboard. When he called for the attack, the mariners sprung up all at once, bursting onto the deck, falling upon the pirates from all sides, screaming murder and vengeance. The battle was fully joined at close quarters with frothing madness and bloody desperation.

Blackbeard was in the midst of it, sweeping over the ship—cutlass in one hand, pistol in the other, cutting apart his enemies as he went. He emptied the pistols in his bandoleer; his daggers were lost in the bodies of his foes. Soon all he had was his cutlass, covered to the hilt in gore. He was slashed across the chest, stabbed in the arm and shot through the cheek. The soldier that embedded his sword in Teach's leg lost his head an instant later. The man who left his dagger protruding from the pirate's back had an arm severed for his effort. Covered in his own blood and the blood of others, bellowing every oath in his prodigiously obscene vocabulary, Blackbeard cut a line to Maynard.

The lieutenant saw the towering Captain Teach bearing down on him, looking no less than the Devil himself. Both men had one loaded pistol left. Both yanked their guns from their belts and fired. Teach missed, but Maynard's ball found its target. Blood sprayed from Teach's chest as the musket ball embedded itself deep in his ribs—a lethal wound that, by all rights, should have felled him where he stood. But it did not even slow Teach down. Covering the distance between Maynard and himself in two huge strides, the dread pirate grabbed Maynard by the forearm with one blood-stained hand and raised his cutlass in the other. The lieutenant tried to fight free, but Blackbeard's grip was as strong as stone. In the last moment, Maynard drew his own cutlass and brought it up to his defense, but in the midst of battle, the pirate's strength was such that he shattered the lieutenant's weapon with one blow.

Maynard stumbled back across the deck, still clutching the now-useless weapon in his hand. Teach took another step forward, his yellowish eyes bulging in boundless fury as he raised the broad blade of his cutlass one more time.

He was born into the world Edward Teach, but his calling to murder and villainy on the clear blue waters of the New World earned him another name. Like many others of his caste, Teach's provenance is disputed. Most histories have him sailing west from anonymous origins in Bristol, England. Other versions label him the son of respectable English colonists in Jamaica or the peninsular Virginian county of Accomack. His true name has also been disputed. He appears in contemporary accounts alternately listed as Tatch, Thatch, Tache and Tash. Some historians claim that these were all versions of an alias and that he was actually christened Edward Drummond. Whatever the case, the issue is academic. Even if no one could say with any certainty what his true name was in the early 18th century, every man who plied Atlantic and Caribbean waters in 1717 and 1718 knew the name Blackbeard all too well. None of them would have concerned themselves too deeply with from what county he hailed.

Rising to become the most feared pirate in the seas, Blackbeard began his maritime career peacefully enough, finding work sailing the West Indies as a merchant seaman. But Louis XIV's open ambitions for the heirless throne in Madrid led to the War of Spanish Succession, and as open hostilities erupted between the French and the English across the colonies, any Englishmen with sea legs willing to indulge in theft and violence were recruited as privateers in the service of Queen Anne.

It is largely believed that Teach volunteered as a privateer sailing out of Jamaica sometime after 1710. He did not seem to have any difficulty making the transition from commerce to violence, discovering a natural talent for terror and bloodshed while boarding French ships in the Caribbean. Yet when peace was negotiated in 1713, Teach suddenly found himself deprived of an outlet for this talent and so pursued what he saw as the only other option for a rum-loving, cutlass-swinging sea dog such as himself.

Teach was not the only sailor about to embrace piracy. In fact, the waters of the New World teemed with out-of-work privateers looking for employment in those busy waters, which buzzed with colonial trade. After years of rapine and excess, many of these sailors were unwilling to return to the grueling work-a-day discipline aboard the merchant ships. Thus the conditions for piracy's much-storied Golden Age were set. All that was needed was a spark.

During the war, English settlements in the Bahamas had suffered repeated raids by French and Spanish forces. Nassau, the capital settlement on New Providence Island, had been plundered and burnt to the ground on three separate occasions. Its population of some 200 families had scattered over the length and breadth of the island, subsisting any way they could. A general lawlessness took over among these distressed inhabitants, which prevailed well after peace had been negotiated. The situation was bad enough to compel the governor of Bermuda to inform London in a report of April 1714, that "three setts of pirates" had emerged from the anarchy on New Providence. The leader of these outlaws was an unknown character by the name of Benjamin Hornigold.

The government in London was not too bothered. New Providence was a tiny settlement on the fringes of the Empire, and the scale of Hornigold's piracy was considered to be of no great concern. His operations were modest, bordering on pathetic, launched from the decks of small boats with crews of no more than 25 men. Thus Hornigold's nest of pirates was spared the immediate attention of the

Royal Navy. Of course the Crown had no way of knowing that Hornigold's small-fry operation would, in just over a year's time, become the festering hub for the next great wave of piracy.

A shipwreck set it off—one of the worst in history. On July 31, 1715, a Spanish treasure fleet of creaking ships, hulls heavy with a fortune in gold and silver, sailed straight into a hurricane off the coast of Florida. Ten ships went to the ocean bottom, along with over 1000 crewmen. And a kingdom's riches lay glittering beneath the waters, along some 40 miles of coastal reef in the Gulf of Mexico. The survivors sent speedy word out to Havana and St. Augustine, and a Spanish salvage expedition was soon under way.

The Spanish were not the only ones to arrive. A king's ransom in bullion lying at the bottom of shallow waters was the kind of news that traveled. Word spread to Bermuda, Carolina, the Bahamas, Jamaica and practically every port in Caribbean waters. It amounted to a nautical gold rush, with every crook, cutthroat and scalawag who could pull on a halyard or hang from a ship's rigging descending on the Florida coast.

One of these men was Captain Henry Jennings, who arrived from Jamaica in command of two good-sized ships and three sloops. He had been sent out with a commission to hunt the waters for pirates but became much more interested in the sunken Spanish treasure. He went so far as to raid a Florida storehouse that contained 120,000 pieces of eight salvaged by the Spanish. Soon after, Jennings apprehended a Spanish ship that was carrying 150,000 pieces of eight from the wreckage site.

Perhaps the recent hostilities with Spain and France had Jennings thinking that the English authorities would overlook his plundering. But this was hardly the case. On his return to Jamaica, he and his crew discovered that they had been branded pirates for their flagrant thievery. With persecution and the gallows looming before them, Jennings and his men decided a change of itinerary would be in their best interest. Shifting sails, they changed their course and sailed on to the Bahamas, where they sought shelter in Hornigold's burgeoning pirate haven.

Jennings was not the only man who had this idea. By the time he arrived, the small nest that the governor of Bermuda had reported in 1714 had already grown, and the following months saw the number of mariner miscreants moored in Hornigold's hideout swell into a society. They came in the wake of Spanish retaliation—when a fleet was sent out to strike against Jennings and the rabble that had swarmed into the region. Ship-borne fortune hunters came flocking to Hornigold's Bahamas to escape Spanish justice. When the Spanish launched attacks of reprisal against former English privateers working illegally as woodcutters in the jungles around Campeche and Honduras,

Hornigold saw a great number of maritime marauders sailing into his coves.

Thus, for the next few years, the Bahamas became the Tortuga and Jamaica for the next generation of pirates, providing safe harbor for ships on the lam, recruiting grounds for captains in need of crews and a trading venue for booty-laden buccaneers. The Bahamas reached their dubious peak in 1716 and 1717, before coordinated English efforts saw the islands largely cleared of these pirate nests. During these years, Benjamin Hornigold also reached the peak of his influence in Caribbean waters, as hundreds of out-of-work privateers flocked to his service.

One of these men was none other than Edward Teach. With no war to sustain him after peace was negotiated, Teach made his way to the Bahamas, where he promptly became Benjamin Hornigold's pernicious protégé. It did not take Teach long to surpass his mentor in the Caribbean pantheon of piracy. Hornigold himself was a temperate man, something of a gentleman pirate who made it a rule to refrain from attacking English ships and tended to refrain from the excessive cruelty many of his peers were famous for. Indeed, by 1718, Hornigold revoked the Jolly Roger. Receiving the appointed governor of the Bahamas with what honors his pirate crew could offer, Hornigold was pardoned, reformed and soon recruited as a pirate hunter.

It is anyone's guess what Hornigold thought of Teach in 1716, when the ambitious privateer docked in New Providence Island looking for work on a pirate vessel. Could he see the madness in the sailor's eyes or any sign of the simmering cruelty and lust for violence that would make him into a legend? Could Hornigold have possibly guessed, that within two years time, his audacious subordinate would have thieved and murdered his way to a career that would totally eclipse his own?

Recruited to serve on Hornigold's 36-gun *Ranger* on an extended campaign of plunder in the West Indies, Teach quickly established himself as the worst of the 145 men onboard. It was more than bravery and an eagerness for violence that set him apart. Teach thrived among the rough men who made their living off high seas robbery. Pirate vessels tended to operate without the formal hierarchies that defined naval and merchant ships of the time. A man's leadership was born from talent, swagger and charisma. There was a sort of code among the men who sailed the fringes: a common zeal for debauchery and daring, a seaborne chauvinism that put great stock in physical power and the quantity of rum a man was able to imbibe and still keep his feet on a rolling deck, a general disgust for gentility and the established conventions of the elite.

The men who best embodied these traits tended to command the most respect. It did not take Teach long to convince the crew of the *Ranger* that there was no man onboard, perhaps over all the Caribbean, with more pirate blood in his veins. Teach looked fierce, spoke fierce, drank fierce and fought fierce. He won the loyalty of a rough and ugly coterie within the *Ranger's* large crew and was soon singled out by Hornigold as well, who gave him the command of a sister-ship with six guns and roughly 70 men. Teach was not idle with his first command.

Late in 1716, Hornigold was at rest, careening the *Ranger* on the Virginia coast after a fruitful expedition in the Caribbean that had amounted to the seizure of many unguarded vessels and a rich bounty in plunder. Successful as Hornigold had been, he was also coming to realize that he did not possess the ruthless sensibilities that were so apparent in some of his crew. Indeed, the mild and merciful Hornigold would have felt ill at ease standing next to Edward Teach. By this time, Hornigold's intemperate subordinate was coming into his own, his thick black beard growing with the madness in his eyes, uglier and more unruly by the day.

Teach was the embodiment of the necessary madness in Hornigold's operation and would get worse after he cut himself off from the tempering influence of his commander. Blackbeard's independence came with the next foray into the West Indies. In early 1717, on the 24th latitude,

Hornigold and his crew came upon the *Concorde*, a French slave ship from St. Malo bound for Martinique. Boarded and captured, the *Concorde* offered generous plunder of gold dust, pieces of eight and jewels, as well as its human cargo. But Teach was far more interested in the ship itself. Solidly built and fast on the water, the French ship was also large enough to mount a significant number of guns. Teach looked at the *Concorde* and saw his future.

Hornigold knew he was in no position to deny his most popular officer when Teach appeared on the *Ranger's* deck requesting command of the captured ship. Teach picked his crew from Hornigold's fiercest, men whose ambitions went no further than rum, booty and freedom on the high seas— ambitions, it turned out, that Hornigold himself no longer shared.

Leaving the French crew aboard Teach's old sloop, the *Ranger* and the *Concorde* sailed back north for New Providence. It was there, in Nassau, where Hornigold announced that he was done as a pirate. Accepting a general pardon issued by the British Crown, Hornigold, along with most of the men who had served on the *Ranger*, swore to never again sail a Jolly Roger and to remain obedient English subjects.

As much as he may have wanted to deny it, Benjamin Hornigold was too much of a gentleman for piracy. The same, however, could not be said

for Edward Teach. Scoffing at Hornigold's reformation, Teach did not have the slightest interest in
pledging obedience to any authority. While Hornigold and his followers were turning themselves in,
he was outfitting his new ship for imminent
depravities. Thus the *Concorde* was renamed the
Queen Anne's Revenge, with 40 cannons mounted at
her gunwales and a horned death's head flying
from the mainmast. Teach was set to steal and
murder his way into legend.

He began right away, breaking one of Hornigold's chief tenets when he captured an English
merchant ship called the *Great Allan* in the waters
off St. Vincent. He was not good about it either.
After stripping the *Great Allan* of its cargo, Teach
forced its crew ashore at St. Vincent and set the
ship on fire. When news of the atrocity reached
Barbados, the governor ordered the 30-gun *Scarborough* to apprehend the outlaws.

When it came to naval engagements between
pirates and the navy, the general rule was that the
pirates did not stick around to test their mettle.
Naval vessels were usually better armed and
stocked with well-trained crews, and few carried
any treasure worth fighting for. More often than
not, pirate ships were equipped for speed over firepower; their crews limited their attacks to vessels
of lesser strength and were not too proud to flee
from the warships that were sent after them. This
was the rule as it applied to most pirates—but
Edward Teach was hardly most pirates.

Squinting through his telescope when the *Scarborough* appeared on the horizon, he could see the British ensign fluttering against the blue sky. It was clearly a naval vessel, a well-equipped man-of-war, and it was moving to intercept. Every man in Teach's crew expected their captain to set full sail and head in the other direction, but there was something in Teach that would not allow him to run. Maybe it was pride, maybe it was madness; maybe this was his way of making a statement—that the waters of the New World had not yet seen the likes of Teach. There had been Henry Morgan and François L'Ollonais; there had been Laurens de Graff and Benjamin Hornigold—but the captain of the *Queen Anne's Revenge* was something new. He was beyond mere plunder and the love of rum, and he did not care an ounce for colonial politics. Here was a man to whom piracy was the ultimate statement of his person, as twisted and depraved as his person was. Piracy amounted to his declaration of war against the civilized world, and he wanted it known that he was not afraid of any authority's agents—not its magistrates, not its priests and certainly not its soldiers.

He did not give the order to flee but instead ordered his men to load the cannons and swing the ship around to meet the approaching *Scarborough*. If any of his sailors thought this madness, it struck them as even crazier to disobey their captain, who was standing against the gunwale, cutlass drawn, eyes wide, sending a roaring string of oaths and curses at the naval vessel. And so the two ships engaged, maneuvering on the wind, trading broadsides, first at long, then medium range. The fight lasted long enough for the captain of the *Scarborough* to appreciate the fact that he was facing an unusually determined pirate who had the full loyalty of his crew. Lacking the fire-power to defeat such a resolved opponent, the *Scarborough* backed off after a few hours, sailing back to Barbados. And for his part, Teach let it get away. He had faced down a warship—that was enough. Word spread quickly after that. There was a new menace on the seas. And his name was Blackbeard.

Teach's infamous alias was born around this time, spread by word of mouth from tavern to tavern. The stories became grander and more frightful as they traveled across the islands. He was a giant, fearless, the Devil himself, with fire running through his veins and a smoldering beard that hung like a tangle of black cord. Teach understood the value of this fearsome reputation and went out of his way to cultivate it. He put lit fuses under his tricorne before engaging ships so that his face was wreathed in black smoke when he boarded his quarry. He devoted an excessive amount of attention to his beard, which he grew long, pleated and tied with brightly colored ribbons. He was big and loud and drank heavily. He berated his men with rum-soaked zeal and never backed away from a fight.

The culture aboard the *Queen Anne's Revenge* was both unhinged and effective, with a captain who loved imitating a demon in command of a ship bent on devilry. Weird stories circulated among the crew. There was one tale of a strange man who sporadically appeared before the sailors, sometimes on deck, sometimes below. No one recognized this man. No one could say who he was, when he had come onboard or why he was there. He was said to vanish as quickly as he appeared, but no one could say where he went. Blackbeard himself did not acknowledge the presence of a mystery passenger. This did not stop the crew from making their own conclusions, taking into account their captain's diabolical behavior and coming up with the seemingly obvious deduction—that the Devil himself was sailing with them.

In his famous 1724 book, *A General History of the Pyrates*, Captain Charles Johnson (a pseudonym, some scholars maintain, for Daniel Defoe) states that many of Blackbeard's crew genuinely believed this to be true. While there can be no accounting for how far an 18th-century pirate went with his superstitions, Blackbeard's bizarre, severe and grossly violent conduct may have convinced the crew that there was some sort of demonic connection.

Once, his ship was becalmed on still winds and lay motionless on the water. There was little more than a breeze for the whole day, leaving Blackbeard and his crew idle and, as the sun crept across the sky, increasingly irritable. It did not take them long to fall back on the rum barrels, and every man was soon good and drunk, including their deranged captain—who was suddenly hit by a novel idea.

"Enough of this damned laying about!" the captain shouted, rum spilling over his cup. "It's time t' see who among ye sorry lot has mettle enough to face what fires await us all in the end." A silence fell over the deck as the pirates took in the fearful sight of their thoroughly soused captain. "What say we go and make a hell of our own, right 'ere on this ship, and see how long we can bear it?"

The silence was broken by a booming voice. "I'll test those fires, captain, and wager ye I can bear 'em better than ye." An ugly pirate stepped from the group on the crowded deck, followed by two more sailors. They were all prominent and ambitious men, each as eager as the next to take their captain's challenge, and in being the best man, rise in the ship's hierarchy.

"That's the spirit, me buckos! The game's afoot!" Blackbeard said, a yellow grin parting the mass of hair over his chin. "Now follow me into the belly, and we'll see what stuff yer made of."

Not knowing what lay ahead, the three pirates followed Blackbeard down into the hold at the very bottom of the ship. They sat down on the ballast boulders as their captain shouted through the dim light. "Bring us down brimstone! Set it afire and bring it down in all our largest pots!" After several huge pots full of smoking sulfur were positioned around the four men, Teach ordered the hatches battened down. Then he fell silent, smiling widely and throwing back his rum as the hold filled with the noxious smoke.

Thus they remained until the choking fumes were so thick they could not see one another in the dim chamber. They held for a little longer and then collapsed all at once, shouting and banging at the hatches, begging to be let out. The sailors above did as they were asked. The men lunged out of the hold, stumbling over themselves to get as far away from the noxious smoke as they could, until they collapsed, coughing and spluttering on the deck. Three men had made this hasty escape. The fourth, Blackbeard himself, was still nowhere to be seen. It took a moment for someone from the crowd to ask the obvious question. "But where's the cap'n?"

"If he's not here, now, in hell for sure," one of the sprawled sailors managed to say. "There was nothing but smoke. There's no man who could 've survived that."

No sooner were the words spoken than Blackbeard emerged from the lower decks, standing sooty and smiling on the sunlit deck, looking as composed as an admiral on Sunday morning, still holding his cup of rum. "What was yer rush, me lads?" he said, finishing the last half of his cup in one swig. "I didn't get a chance to finish me rum."

One of the awestruck sailors spoke up. "But cap'n, ye look as if ye were coming straight from the gallows."

To which Teach gave his famous reply: "Me lad, that's a right brilliant idea. The next time we'll play at gallows and see who can swing longest on the noose." Needless to say, no one, not the men still hacking away, nor the stunned witnesses, dared take Blackbeard up on this challenge.

Not all of the pirate captain's tests were so jocular. One night, he was in his cabin playing cards with two of his shipmates—a trusted and loyal friend named Israel Hands and another man whose name history has forgotten. They were in the middle of a hand when Teach, without warning and for no apparent reason, reached into his belt, pulled two pistols, cocked them and trained the weapons on the card players, arms crossed underneath the table. He had moved so fast that neither man had time to react until he blew out the candle. Only then, when the room was suddenly black, were the two men able to take stock of the situation.

The nameless man sprang from the table, knocking his chair over in his haste as he ran for the door. Israel Hands, however, did not budge, but remained fixed to his chair, perhaps assuming that his captain was bluffing, testing which of the two men had the greater sand.

He was wrong. The cabin lit up with the flash of powder as Blackbeard discharged both his pistols at the same time. The man who had run escaped harm, but Hands received a lead ball in the knee as a reward for his sturdiness, a wound that he survived but that would leave him with an ugly limp for the rest of his life. As the bleeding sailor was carried from his cabin, the crew could not help but wonder why Blackbeard would shoot one of his closest friends. Someone gathered the courage to ask the question.

Blackbeard turned to the man and said, "Well, me bucko, if I didn't kill one of ye every now and then, you'd forget who I was, now wouldn't ye?"

For a time, the rule by terror tactic worked well for the pirate. He enjoyed remarkable success in the Caribbean. In May 1717, soon after he had fought off the *Scarborough*, Blackbeard came upon the ship commanded by Stede Bonnet, a Barbadian planter of genteel origins who had recently turned pirate. Bonnet was more than a little awed at his meeting with the already famous Blackbeard and gladly took up his offer of partnership.

Stede Bonnet was an anomaly within the fraternity of pirates. A distinguished and successful plantation owner who had made no small fortune growing sugar cane on Barbados, he fit in easily with the island's plantation society. Far better, anyway, than with the rough buccaneers he suddenly decided to throw his lot in with. Everyone who knew him was taken completely by surprise when, seemingly out of nowhere, he outfitted a sloop with 10 guns and 70 unsavory sailors and pushed out to sea in search of booty. Stede Bonnet had called his ship the *Revenge*, but no one had the slightest notion what, exactly, he was seeking vengeance for. He had been so well esteemed on Barbados that, even after news of his attacks reached the island, people tended to pity rather than loathe him. Certainly the man they knew could not be responsible for such deeds, went the conventional wisdom. He must have fallen ill of some disorder of the mind. And it was generally prophesied that the whole affair was sure to end in tragedy, for there was no way that a man of such undeniably proper roots could ever win any real respect or authority in the world of ruffians he had chosen to embrace.

The truth of this was made plain shortly after Bonnet fell in with the *Queen Anne's Revenge*, when Blackbeard unceremoniously relieved the former plantation owner of his command and put up one of his own officers, a man remembered only as Richards. To his credit, Blackbeard did go out of his way to explain the situation to the deposed captain, inviting Bonnet to his ship and taking him into the privacy of his cabin. "Y 'see, matey, I've kept a keen eye on the way ye run yer ship and can tell ye now that it takes something to keep salts like these in tow—something that ye don't have." Blackbeard raised his hand at the protest that was beginning to form in Bonnet's mouth. "Now it's clear to me that the captain's coat is hanging a bit heavy on yer shoulders, so why wear it? Consider this an invitation, me bucko. You'll be a guest on this here ship, living easy without the cares and duties of command." So Stede Bonnet was essentially made a captive on Blackbeard's ship, and not one man aboard his sloop uttered a single word of protest.

Over the next few months, the *Queen Anne's Revenge* and Bonnet's confiscated *Revenge* enjoyed great fortune in the Caribbean, working together as they took a general eastward course, boarding and robbing a good number of merchant vessels along the way. Blackbeard's reputation increased with each raid, so that by the time he reached the Leeward Islands, the governor there dared not risk sea travel without a heavily armed escort.

By January 1718, Blackbeard had steered into more northerly waters, and his two ships were moored in a North Carolina inlet. He had not been guided there by a capricious wind. Teach, as shrewd as he was vicious, was in North Carolina for a reason—Governor Charles Eden. Teach went before the colonial authority in Bath and, with his closest crewmen, submitted to the good grace of the Crown and took advantage of the latest general pardon to swear off piracy and become an honest sailor.

Of course, Teach had no intention of giving up piracy. The surrender was all a show, a deal struck with North Carolina's corrupt governor in which the pirate hoped to gain legitimacy and shelter from the law in exchange for some of his booty. Thus the port of Bath in North Carolina became a base of operations for Teach—the only jurisdiction in all the colonies where he was welcomed as a law-abiding citizen instead of the murdering marauder that he was.

After straightening out his situation in North Carolina, Blackbeard returned to the West Indies, spending the early months of 1718 sowing more terror in those waters. In the Bay of Honduras, he managed to capture several ships. Some were merely emptied of their treasure and sent on their way. Those considered fast and large enough Blackbeard converted into pirate ships and added them to his flotilla. A Jamaican sloop called the *Adventure* was captured; her captain and entire crew were pressed into Blackbeard's service and put under the command of their new commander, Israel Hands. Another sloop taken alongside four other vessels was considered pirate-worthy and was recruited into service. Before long, Teach was in command of nothing less than a miniature fleet, with his *Queen Anne's Revenge*, three other sizeable sloops and several tenders that buzzed between them. He had over 400 sailors manning these ships.

Many more vessels were destroyed outright. When Blackbeard and his men captured a merchant ship called the *Protestant Caesar*, they took great offense to the fact that it was from Boston, where a great number of pirates had recently been hanged. After the *Protestant Caesar's* crew abandoned ship at the sight of approaching pirates, Blackbeard ordered the ship be put to the torch. After a period of nursing his wounded pride, Stede Bonnet began to rise to some prominence onboard Blackbeard's ship. The *Revenge's* jilted captain cultivated a vendetta against his island home, and a number of captured Barbadian sloops were set afire.

While they careened and rested in the innumerable coves and cays across the Caribbean and more than once deposited their booty in Havana, Blackbeard's fleet never abandoned the idea that their base was in North Carolina. Of all the rivers, inlets and capes where they dropped anchor, the coves of the Ocracoke Inlet became their favorite hideout.

Not that Teach was taking great pains at anonymity. Indeed, he plundered American waters with the same absence of compunction and concern as was his habit in the Caribbean. In May 1718, he dropped anchor at the entrance of Charleston harbor, South Carolina, and boarded every ship that came and went. Blackbeard's fleet ended up capturing well over a dozen vessels. It brought all shipping traffic out of Charleston to a complete standstill and captured a council member and extracted a ransom from the governor of the colony. By the time Blackbeard weighed anchor and moved on, the authorities in South Carolina were clamoring for justice.

But Teach moved well beyond their jurisdiction. He sailed south to the West Indies before heading to the safety of North Carolina, where he was formally acknowledged as a law-abiding sailor. It was then, while mooring in the Topsail Inlet in June 1718, that Teach pulled one of the most audacious moves of his career. The scheme began when the *Queen Anne's Revenge* and another one of his sloops, commanded by Israel Hands, were run aground on their way to careening. Immobile in the inlet, Blackbeard roared curses up and down his deck while berating his sailors for their incompetence. But it was all show, for Teach had deliberately grounded the vessels.

Despite Blackbeard's reign of terror, ugly divisions had begun to crop up among his sailors. The problem was that his fleet had grown too large to sustain itself. Even with their many successes at sea, there were too many men sailing under Blackbeard's banner, so that each man received a paltry division of the booty and was growing increasingly bitter about it. Rancor spread throughout the fleet, and the pirates' loyalties were split. One group was making mutinous plans. There may have been a level of madness in Blackbeard's cruelty, but he was not so insane that he did not see what was going on around him. When the situation grew so bad that open fights were erupting between the factions, their captain decided it was time to take action.

Only a select group of 40 or so sailors were in on the plan when Blackbeard proclaimed a newfound confidence in Stede Bonnet's ability to captain a pirate ship. Flushing with pride, Bonnet was given back the command of the *Revenge*, along with the advice that he make the trek to Bath and obtain the same pardon Blackbeard himself had received from Governor Eden. The moment Bonnet had set off, Teach and his selected crew began to load the fleet's treasure onto the *Adventure*. Then, without warning, Teach announced to roughly 320 pirates that he was no longer in need of their services, and that they could take the two beached ships and do whatever they pleased with them. Not parting with a single piece of treasure, Blackbeard and his 40 sailors then boarded the *Adventure* and departed, their holds heavy with booty and rum.

Shedding the mutinous mass of pirates, Blackbeard sailed forth lean and rich, in command of a staunchly loyal crew, with the misappropriated wealth of 400 robbers in the hands of 40 men.

They sailed back to their favorite haunts in the Ocracoke Inlet. Teach once more approached Governor Eden to surrender to the King's clemency and obtain a pardon from the colony. Swayed less by Blackbeard's contrition than he was by a portion of his booty, Eden once again granted the pirate a pardon.

Over the next few months, Blackbeard alternated between far-ranging expeditions and exorbitant binges of lavish dissolution in North Carolina. The governor of Pennsylvania issued a warrant for his arrest in August 1718 after Blackbeard was spotted drunk beyond reason on the streets of Philadelphia. Blackbeard raided English ships from the North American colonies in the Atlantic. He relieved French ships of cargoes of spices, sugar and tobacco in the waters around Bermuda.

Returning to the inlets of North Carolina, Blackbeard made it his habit to drown himself in the pleasures of the flesh. He bought a grand manse in Bath and ingratiated himself to the richest colonists. He bought his place in high society with his excessive and ostentatious parties. Neighboring plantation owners regularly received gifts of sugar and rum and took special pleasure in befriending the one and only Blackbeard, with his rough manners and dubious celebrity.

Yet it was not long before the novelty of Blackbeard's presence gave way to the realities of having such a man as a neighbor. His crew began coming into Bath more regularly, swaggering through the town loud and drunk, without the slightest concern for manners or conventions. They crowded into the taverns, drinking the establishments dry and spilling onto the streets, insulting and abusing anyone they came across, with no regard for status or sex.

Teach became temporarily enamored with a local girl of 16 years, who he courted with an avalanche of gold, jewels and fine silks. Governor Eden himself attended the wedding. Some sources even suggest that the governor performed the ceremony. But it would not be a happy coupling. It soon emerged that Teach already had 14 wives—all of them still living—scattered across the colonies. He also had an ugly habit of "lending" the poor girl to his favorite sailors. The details of such transactions are not suitable for these pages. Nor were they acceptable to Bath townsfolk, but by this time, no man in town dared to openly voice any issue with Blackbeard.

It was not long before they too were made to suffer degradations at the hands of the resident pirate. Blackbeard's lifestyle was so exorbitant that even his considerable fortune was unable to sustain it. Families who had so recently been lavished with gifts were now having their homes routinely ransacked by Teach's men. Even as their valuables were stolen to finance the lifestyle of Teach and his crew, no one dared raise any complaint, and Governor Eden did not press a single charge against the pirate.

But while the authorities in North Carolina did nothing to stop Blackbeard, Governor Spotswood of Virginia did not share Eden's appreciation for the pirate. Virginia traders had suffered from Blackbeard's operations as much as those of the surrounding colonies. The proximity of the pirate hideout in Ocracoke caused a buzz throughout the colony. It always became news when a former member of Blackbeard's crew was apprehended somewhere in the colony. More than a few of these ex-pirates were wandering into Virginia, usually popping up in stories of disorder or violence in local taverns. Many of these men were arrested as pirates but could not be legally prosecuted when they produced proof of the King's pardon, signed by Governor Eden.

Everyone knew that Teach himself was living in North Carolina and, despite having accepted Eden's pardon, was still raiding freely up and down the coast. He had successfully eluded capture on open water, and, thanks to Governor Eden's protection, was essentially untouchable while moored in North Carolina. No one was happy about having the worst pirate the colonies had ever seen based so close. When a rumor got out that Blackbeard was planning to fortify the Ocracoke and make it into a general haven for other vessels sailing under a black flag, Governor

Spotswood decided Blackbeard had to be stopped, even if he enjoyed the protection of the corrupt Governor Eden.

Because their mission was a contravention of colonial law, Maynard and Baker had taken great pains to maintain secrecy as they sailed their two sloops south along the North Carolina coast. Still, quiet as they were, their appearance in the Ocracoke Inlet in the afternoon of November 21 was no surprise to Teach. He had received a letter from the secretary of the colony warning him that Spotswood had taken a great interest in the situation in Ocracoke and would likely be sending out an expedition. This was precisely what the pirate assumed the two sloops were when they pulled into the inlet.

So it was two ships against one, with Teach in command of a bare crew of no more than 25 men. And yet in spite of such odds, he did not appear to be concerned in the least. When he saw that Maynard and Baker had given the order to drop anchor, he ordered the rest of the ship's rum be brought up. While a somber silence reigned upon the two naval vessels at the mouth of the inlet, the *Adventure* was alive with raucous cavorting. The way the opening hours of the battle went the next morning, it quickly became apparent that Blackbeard's pirates, drunk and outnumbered as they were, were still more than able to defeat the Virginian mariners.

In the end, the battle hinged on a single moment, the action of a split second, which came after the *Adventure* had effectively disabled Baker's *Ranger* and cut down the bulk of Maynard's crew with a broadside of grapeshot; after Blackbeard's men had swung aboard Maynard's sloop and were surprised by the stiff counterattack that surged up from below deck; after the desperate close quarters battle that saw pirate and mariner engaged with pistols, cutlasses and daggers, or, when there was nothing else, throttling one another with their bare hands; after Blackbeard strode across the blood-soaked deck toward its captain, leaving a trail of bodies behind him; and after Maynard shot him square in the chest and the looming pirate, bleeding from dozens of wounds, raised his cutlass to cut down the lieutenant who had come for his head. In that moment, if Blackbeard's blade had been allowed to fall, the battle aboard the sloop might have easily turned in favor of the *Adventure's* heartened pirates. But Teach's blow never landed. For in that moment, one of Maynard's men leapt behind Blackbeard and brought his own cutlass down across the pirate captain's throat, slashing open his jugular and sending him toppling to the deck, dead.

The battle aboard the sloop ended with Blackbeard's death. Those pirates not slain either surrendered immediately or leapt overboard in a desperate bid to escape, only to be shot to death while trying to swim away. On board the *Adventure*, a pirate named Caesar, who Blackbeard had ordered to ignite the ship's magazine if the battle should turn against them, was wrestled to the ground before he was able to execute Teach's command.

The fight was over. The legendary Blackbeard lay on Maynard's deck, soaked through in his own blood. The cost had been high. Ten mariners lay dead and 25 wounded, one of which later succumbed to his injuries. Nine pirates were dead, while the remaining nine were wounded.

There would be one more depravity on Ocracoke Inlet that day. Ordering the captured pirates to be locked in the brig, Maynard promptly beheaded Blackbeard and had the pirate's head hoisted up on the bowsprit. The pirate's body was then dumped into the bloodied waters around the sloop. Even his headless body was a source of awe. A few of the sailors present later swore they saw it swim once around the sloop before it sank to the bottom.

And then Blackbeard was gone. Maynard returned to Virginia victorious, with Blackbeard's head swinging before him. The lieutenant collected his reward, while the gruesome trophy served as a warning for many years, mounted high over the entrance to the Hampton River, which would come to be called Blackbeard's Point—a reminder to all of the fate of those who dared sail under the Jolly Roger.

CHAPTER FIVE

Rackham, Bonny and Read

AN IMAGE OF THE PIRATE captain exists in the popular imagination. He is a rum-swilling, swashbuckling braggart of casual cruelty and zealous avarice, who is as protective of his freedom as he is bound to his hedonism. With a tricorne perched jauntily over a tight bandana, a cutlass hanging from his waist and pistols bristling from his belts and sashes, he appraises the world around him with lusty eyes—or, rather, a lusty *eye*, for the other is usually hidden beneath a black eye patch. Of course, he goes nowhere without his pet parrot perched upon his shoulder.

While writers like Robert Louis Stevenson gave life to this Long John Silver-like icon, that image is not the only pirate stereotype that exists in our culture. The lives of pirates have been romanticized at least as much as they have been vilified. For every bloodthirsty Captain Hook or Long John Silver, there is also a Captain Peter Blood. A dashing Errol Flynn, with a cutlass, swings from the rigging and makes ladies swoon with his good looks, noble intentions and fearless heroics.

By all accounts, "Calico" John Rackham did not suffer from any excess of fearless heroics or noble intentions, but his association with two of the most famous female seafarers of his time has done much to cement his place in legend as a piratical lothario. While not all biographies of Rackham paint him as such, there is a tradition among certain writers to present him as a vain and mostly anemic buccaneer, whose luck with women and attention to wardrobe far surpassed his ability to effectively lead a ship of thieves.

There is no clear record of when Rackham was born, where he came from or how he arrived in the Caribbean. He emerged from complete anonymity late in 1718, the quartermaster of a pirate ship commanded by one Captain Charles Vane.

Vane himself was a man of some distinction, earning his place in the piratical pantheon a year before for his defiance against Woodes Rogers, the first royally appointed governor of the Bahamas. Rogers' arrival in Nassau was a pivotal moment in the Bahamas' history. A lawless den of piracy for years, Nassau was said to be headquarters to some 2000 pirates when Rogers sailed in at the head of three Royal men-of-war, in the summer of 1718. Rogers readied himself for the worst and lined up his ships for battle. But it was a battle that never came. The pirates of Nassau capitulated to royal authority with very little issue, the majority of them accepting the general pardon Rogers brought with him, which granted amnesty to all local sailors for any crime if they swore off future piracy and pledged their loyalty to the Crown.

Captain Charles Vane was the one notable exception. Deciding he was not ready to conclude his pirating career, Vane gathered together a crew of like-minded sailors and prepared his sloop to sail from Nassau. Not before making a statement to the new governor, however. Vane was ready when Rogers' ships appeared in Nassau's harbor. The pirate ordered a recently captured French brigantine he had no use for set on fire and cut from its moorings. Fearing the flaming ship might be packed with explosives, the naval vessels steered clear, and the brigantine cut a path through Roger's formation. Vane's speedy sloop was close behind, riding in the wake of the unmanned decoy, fast on the wind, black flag flying high in open defiance. When it became apparent what was going on, Rogers gave the order to pursue, but Vane's sloop was faster and more maneuverable than the bulky men-of war that came after him. Thus Vane was able to give Rogers the slip in front of the whole town of Nassau, adding a small round of audacious cannon fire as he flew past the governor's vessel.

A daring feat, no doubt, enough to make any glory-seeking pirate at least a little envious. The stunt marked Vane's highpoint. The rest of his career was notably devoid of any laurels, unfolding for the most part as a chain of one humiliating incident after another, until he found himself hanging by the neck at Gallows Point, Port Royal, less than a year after his escape from Nassau.

John Rackham's story begins with Vane's greatest defeat. It was late November 1718, and Vane and his men were sailing in the Atlantic. They had enjoyed only modest success since they had sailed from the Bahamas, and Vane seemed to have brought an arrogance to his post that alienated many of his men. Indeed, by the time they came upon the French vessel that precipitated Vane's downfall, the pirates serving under him may well have been looking for the slightest excuse to rebel.

Vane's indecision was the excuse. Appraising a French vessel from a distance, the pirate captain deemed it safe pickings. He called all hands to deck, put full sails to the wind and ordered his helmsman to intercept. Yet as they drew closer to their quarry, Vane immediately began to think twice about the situation. Up close, the ship looked much bigger and better manned that it had seemed from a distance. When the captain spied the row of gun ports, open and ready, he made up his mind. This was no hapless merchant they were bearing down upon, but a battle-ready man-of-war. Any attempt at boarding would be nothing less than suicide. He immediately ordered his men to stand down and had the helmsman disengage from the chase.

Controversy immediately erupted aboard the vessel, as a vocal group of sailors, desperate for booty, began to shout that Vane was being too cautious—they could take the French ship. Despite the uproar, their captain did not budge. As they turned and sailed away, he insisted that the ship was a man-of-war with more firepower and more men than his ship had. It was a fight they would not win. "Even if they don't sink us on our approach, they'll run us out by strength of arms," Vane insisted to his angry men.

Yet the crew would not let the matter go. Vane had the support of some 15 sailors and the first mate, but the rest were adamant that their captain had made the wrong decision. Not only in this instance, but in many others before. It seems that Rackham, the quartermaster, emerged as the leader of the angry faction, which decided the next day that Vane's authority should stand to a vote of confidence.

History does not tell us if Rackham was an ambitious man who led the opposition against Vane to seize command of the ship, or if he was elevated to the position by the spontaneous acclaim of the men. Whatever the case, the issue of leadership came to a decision between Vane and his quartermaster, John Rackham. Gathered on the deck, the sailors cast their votes and counted. On November 24, 1718, the ship quartermaster was made into the captain. Charles Vane and those loyal to him were put upon a recently captured, dismally small sloop, while Rackham sailed away with his first command.

There is very little information about who Rackham was before he became a captain. Much is made of his penchant for bright, flamboyant dress—his alias, "Calico Jack," arising from his favorite fabric. Rackham would have not been the only pirate commander guilty of a level of vanity. A certain opulence in dress was one of the ways captains often distinguished themselves from their crew—a tricorne instead of a bandana, high boots instead of bare feet, a military greatcoat instead of a sailor's tunic. Yet Rackham's extravagance went well beyond the typical vanities. Did any of his shipmates wonder at their captain's insistence on wearing clean and brightly colored calico? Or the way he never appeared on deck without carefully coiffed hair, his moustache and beard always clean and combed? Where there was no shortage of reeking, toothless, drunk, jaundiced and scurvy-ridden sailors, Calico Jack's concern for appearance and personal hygiene surely raised eyebrows. It turned out that there was indeed an explanation for their captain's fastidiousness, but the reason would not come to light until the very end, when he and his men, shackled before a Jamaican magistrate, stood to receive the final sentence for their crimes.

Well-groomed as he was, Rackham proved himself to be somewhat middling when it came to piracy. Possessed with neither driving ambition nor any exceptional lust for violence, Rackham did not orchestrate any grand campaigns in the short time he was captain. Consistently coming upon just enough plunder to stay afloat, he came nowhere near the kind of notoriety attached to vicious seadogs like Blackbeard and Edward Low. The place he earned in history did not spring from any travesties committed on the seaways of the New World.

Rather, it was the bizarre goings-on that transpired on the ship he commanded. Two crew members lead scandalous lives which compromised 18th-century English assumptions of the respective roles and temperaments—of the fundamental differences in character—between men and women. That there was a fraternity of corrupt sailors who took up arms for murder and theft on the seas was detestable to proper society. Piracy repugnant? Certainly. Yet given the history of maritime violence that had been a fact of life for centuries, while it was detestable, it could hardly be said to be unexpected. That a number of these corrupt sailors in the 18th century might be women, however (and *English* women, at that), was something else altogether. It was an impossibility, an aberration. Women were supposed to be the gentler sex, the mothers of succeeding generations, the bedrock of proper civilization. And yet on John Rackham's ship, there was not one cutlass-wielding female, but two.

To what extent are our personalities inherited, in the blood, immutable as our bones? And how much are we shaped by our environment, the values, expectations and pressures of the world into which we are born? The question of nature versus nurture seems especially pertinent when one considers the life of a character as extreme as Anne Bonny. What impelled a planter's daughter to leave a life of wealth and comfort to cast her fortune into the sea? Anne Bonny's slide into maritime perfidy began with her love for a sailor. Or, at least, love was the explanation she gave her father when the incredulous Virginian planter demanded to know why she was throwing her life away to board a ship bound for the Caribbean. With a woman as tempestuous as Anne Bonny, however, love was not the most reliable of motives.

Born in Ireland, Anne was the illegitimate product of a passionate union between her father, a town barrister in County Cork, and one of his household maids. The birth of Anne Bonny was not the only outcome of the affair, which also left her father divorced, publicly disgraced and cut-off from his mother's inheritance. Nevertheless, attorney and maid shared a genuine bond. Despite what it did to his professional prestige and standing in the community, the barrister took his mistress in and openly raised his daughter out of wedlock. While the behavior of the father was nothing compared to the crimes his daughter would one day be charged with, his scandalous young family did irreparable damage to his reputation. He eventually lost his practice and was forced to look elsewhere for a means to support his wife and daughter.

His gaze fell upon the colonies across the Atlantic. Thinking he was leaving a life of scandal and disrepute behind, he settled in the Carolinas, where he promptly went from practicing law to running his own plantation. His enterprises were well rewarded, and Anne Bonny grew up knowing all the comforts of America's highest caste.

Anne's father doted on his daughter, who was as pretty and spirited as she was stubborn and rebellious. Her mother died when Anne was still young, so Anne was compelled to take over the running of the household at an early age. The task was well within her abilities, but she had a vicious temper, which she occasionally unleashed on her servants when they displeased her. Some accounts suggest that she might have even stabbed a servant to death, but this was never confirmed beyond rumor. Another often-told episode from her early life in Carolina has her beating senseless a lecher who tried to force himself upon her

Violent and willful as Anne was, her father invested all his hopes in her—hopes that were dashed when she turned 16 and informed him that she had fallen in love with a broke sailor named James Bonny and that she intended to marry him. One might expect that Anne's father would have been sympathetic to his daughter's passions, given the course of events that had brought him to Carolina. Yet what was acceptable for the father was anything but for the daughter. He tried to reason with her, to no avail. He forbade the union. Anne became more determined to see her lover. He threatened the sailor with his life. She married the seaman and sailed away.

Anne Bonny may have inherited passion from her father, but the origins of her legendary caprice are a mystery, perhaps born on tropical waters with her first taste of freedom on the briny wind. Wherever her capriciousness came from, it took hold of her soon after she and her new husband arrived in the Bahamas. The journey south was not kind to the couple. Very little remained between them after the shine of first passion faded. Anne had grown used to a life of luxury. James was unable to provide it. Anne was willful and fiercely independent. James was a shipman, shaped by discipline and obedience.

Disembarking in Nassau when it was still a wild pirate's haven, Anne was immediately taken with the madness of the worst taverns. Among the roaring personalities of the sea-robbers, she promptly forgot about her husband and fell in love again after meeting a dashing young buccaneer with clean hair and bright calico clothing. John Rackham was equally taken with pretty young Anne. In a matter of days, the two were conspiring about a way to spend the rest of their lives together.

Not that Anne's marriage was any issue. Indeed, the rash girl did not give her nuptials a second thought. There was no law or social sanction to fall afoul of among the wild islands of Bahamas. As far as she was concerned, James Bonny no longer existed. Rather, the problem lay on Rackham's side. He was a pirate, after all, and knowing his fellow crewmen well, he did not relish the idea of bringing fair Anne onboard as a passenger.

For Anne's part, Rackham's profession was what attracted her most to him. In Nassau, she became enamored with the idea of the pirate's life and found that, more than anything else, she wanted to be on the deck of a renegade ship, plundering at will and sowing terror among honest seafarers. It spoke loudly to her fiercely independent soul—so loudly, in fact, that the headstrong teenager decided she would join Rackham's crew. Despite the restrictions popular convention put on a woman with such ambitions, she became determined to know what it was like to hold a cutlass to a man's throat and demand his gold. She would be a woman pirate.

But she also decided that it would be prudent not to be so open about the "woman" part. Recruiting herself to the ship Rackham was serving on, Anne did not board with dress and jewelry, but rather took great pains to disguise the fact that she was a woman. She tied her hair into a bandana and wore her shirts and pants baggy beneath an oversized greatcoat that hid every trace of her figure. If anyone onboard thought for a moment that there was the possibility a woman might be among them, Anne's boyish disguise might not have held up. But, because Rackham's fellows could not comprehend the idea of a woman choosing to sail with a gang of pirates, Anne was able to remain incognito.

The dates of her piratical provenance are unclear. It is not known exactly when Anne became Rackham's partner in piracy. She definitely was not in New Providence for any great length of time before embarking upon her first foray as a freebooter. And she arrived in Nassau when it was still infested with black flags, before Woodes Rogers established order in 1718. Whatever the case, she was certainly by Rackham's side in the summer of that year, under the command of Charles Vane when he openly defied the future governor and ran the Nassau blockade while flying the Jolly Roger.

The danger and chaos of the freebooting life did little to compromise Rackham and Bonny's relationship. Indeed, remarkably, it seems the couple thrived off the violence, plunder and secrecy. No one guessed that the young pirate always standing firmly by Rackham's side was actually a woman. In time, the newcomer proved to be among the most able robbers aboard the ship. It turned out that Bonny was nothing less than gifted. Quickly growing skillful with a cutlass, she was a zealous and courageous raider with a glaring streak of cruelty that earned her the admiration of her colleagues. Her natural ability at boarding and robbing soon made her one of the most popular pirates onboard—until her feats threatened to overshadow Rackham himself.

Given her ardor for violence, it is likely that Bonny was one of the driving forces behind Captain Vane's overthrow. Certainly his order to turn and run from potential quarry, whether a wise move or not, would not have sat well with Anne Bonny. It is even likely that she had ambitions to depose Vane and take command herself. If so, it is apparent that this is where the audacious young woman, perhaps for the first time in her life, drew a line that she would not cross. The awareness of what a ship of pirates might think if they discovered they were taking orders from a teenage girl was enough to curb Bonny's aspirations.

So she did the next best thing and threw her weight behind Rackham's captaincy, her significant influence helping to make her dandyish beau into captain. Not that the appointment did anything to increase Rackham's stature in Bonny's eyes. In fact, it seems the following months saw the young woman grow increasingly disenchanted with her lover. Rackham's uninspired command did much to dim her dreams of glory and riches, no matter how well groomed and brightly dressed her captain was.

After taking control of Vane's ship in November 1718, Rackham gave the order to sail south to the

Caribbean. The pirates won their first prize under Rackham's command that same year, coming across a small ship on the windward side of Jamaica. It was a modest haul, consisting mostly of enough rum and victuals to supply a Christmas celebration on a small island of the Lesser Antilles, which went on for several weeks. Drunk and idle under the tropical sun, the pirates only ventured back out to sea when their stores began to run out. The early months of 1719 saw them sailing on to the Bahamas with very little luck. They captured and then lost an English ship laden with prisoners bound for the sugar plantations. They also captured and then promptly lost two vessels in the Bahamas.

It was at about this time that the men aboard the ship began to notice that everyone's favorite mate, Bonny, was beginning to swell around the middle. No one suspected anything beyond extra rations. It was plainly visible, after all, that Bonny was the captain's favorite sailor. No one would have been surprised to learn that the young pirate was enjoying extra rations. Because none suspected for a moment the truth of Bonny's concealed sex, no one hit upon the fact that she was actually in the early stages of pregnancy.

Fixated as she was on her cruel passions, Bonny was hardly prepared to take on the mantle of motherhood. She desired the pirate's life more than anything else and sought a quick and tidy resolution to her condition. Rackham did the best he could, sailing to a small settlement on the Cuban coast, where he was close to a family that he could trust to keep his first mate's identity a secret. The resolution was neither quick nor tidy. While Rackham departed, promising Bonny that he would return after she had been given enough time to deliver her child, the young woman was left in the quiet fishing town, going half-crazy with idleness as her belly swelled. When she finally gave birth, Bonny abandoned her child without a second thought, putting on her costume again and rejoining Rackham's crew upon their dutiful return.

If Bonny was at all resentful of Rackham for having inflicted her with a child, her antipathy grew when she learned how little he had accomplished in her absence. By now it was blatantly obvious that her dashing young Captain John Rackham was no Blackbeard. No grand battles, no booty worth talking about, no stories of adventure—Rackham had added to his shoddy showing by sailing to Nassau to accept the king's pardon and obtain a letter of marque against the Spanish from Governor Rogers. Thus he was not even a pirate anymore, but a privateer, in the service of the Crown against the Spanish. Bonny could now plainly see how far Rackham stood from the daring and hell-bent rogue she had imagined in her love. Nevertheless, there were no other freebooters around to join, so Bonny took her place next to her underachieving pirate and set sail again in search of booty and adventure. There is no

record of what became of the child she left behind
in Cuba.

It was at around this time that Rackham conducted what might have been his most daring
operation. They were still in Cuban waters when
they came upon a well-armed Spanish ship sailing
with a recently captured English sloop. It was the
Cuban coast guard, who immediately identified
Rackham as an interloper and set upon his ship.
Neither Bonny nor any other pirate aboard Rackham's vessel believed for a second that they had
a fighting chance against such a well-armed ship.
They threw their backs into Rackham's call for
evasive action.

A close and desperate chase followed, where the
pirates came under heavy fire maneuvering
between the Cuban coast and a rocky islet a mile or
two from shore. The pirates escaped immediate
destruction, but the day did not end well. Rackham's ship was cornered in a little cove in the islet,
while the Spanish ship was poised at the edge of
the channel in position to pulverize them the next
morning. Fully aware that they were doomed if
they were still there at day's first light, Rackham
gave the order for silence when the sun went down,
telling his crew to arm themselves with cutlasses
and pistols and crowd into a single boat.

Without any torch to guide them, the whole of
Rackham's crew made their way in the darkness
through the water, creeping by the Spanish ship

and around the islet to the channel where the English sloop was anchored. They made no sound as they climbed up onto the sloop, overwhelming the skeleton crew without firing a shot. The pirates held their cutlasses to the Spaniards' throats as Rackham issued the warning—any sound or signal to the coast guard on the other side of the islet would spell the death of them all.

At first light, the eager Spaniards bore down on the vessel anchored off the islet, opening a crippling round of fire that tore gaping holes in the hull and ripped up the rigging. It did not take them long to figure out they were firing on a deserted ship. Immediately sailing into the channel between the islet and the mainland, they confirmed their worst fears—the pirates had escaped on the captured sloop and were far beyond reach.

The daring escape certainly bolstered Rackham's prestige among his crew, but the humble scale of their subsequent raids did little to repair his standing with Anne Bonny. While trolling the waters off Jamaica and Hispaniola, their plunder was minor, limited to tenders and fishing boats. The day's catch and a fisherman's tackle were not the kind of riches Bonny was interested in. More and more, she equated her captain with fishing nets and frustration. Her eyes began to wander.

There was one young man in particular that caught her attention. Smooth-faced and imbued with a nonchalant grace, he stood out among the loud and ugly sailors under Rackham's command. He spoke very little and did not drown himself in the rum barrels with the zeal that was the fashion with the pirates of the time. Yet youthful and reserved as he was, there was something about the mysterious buccaneer that warned the more boorish sailors away—a seriousness in his look and manner that made it clear he was not to be trifled with. And whenever there was a call for action, he was at the forefront, conducting himself with skill and courage.

The sailors, respecting the young pirate's restraint and reticence, tended to leave him alone, but Bonny was intrigued and went out of her way to befriend him. If she had met him anywhere else, the impulsive woman would not have bothered with too much of a preamble of friendship. She had always acted on the spark of first attraction. This was where she was headed with her new interest, but there were issues she had to contend with at sea.

First there was Rackham. Even though her interest was waning, the captain of the ship was still very much in love. Bonny knew he would not look kindly on her taking another man. Also there were only so many places onboard a sloop where two regular sailors could conduct a relationship unseen. Second, there was the issue of her identity. As far as the object of her affection was concerned, Bonny was a man. How would she reveal the fact that she was a woman? And how would she be able to seduce him as such if she was forced to walk around as a boy all of the time? Finally, would she be able to trust the young man with her secret? What if he were to suddenly shed his reticence upon learning the incredible secret? A lot of questions, which even the rash Anne Bonny would have considered before acting on her passions. So she considered them and pursued the pirate nonetheless, spending as much time in his company as she could when Rackham was not looking, scheming about how she would reveal her identity and intentions.

In due time, Bonny found ways to overcome all these difficulties and presented herself to the young man below deck one night. The ship was anchored off some Caribbean island. Rackham and his crew were drunk beyond reason up above. It was on this night, after some awkward fumbling in the darkness below deck, that Anne Bonny discovered one more difficulty existed. A complication greater than anything she might have anticipated, which essentially made their union impossible. That complication was this: the mysterious pirate, like Anne Bonny, was a woman in disguise.

For Mary Read, passing herself off as a boy in the company of men was no great thing; she had been doing it for much of her life. Mary was born in England, the circumstances of her origins just as difficult as that of her counterpart. Mary's mother was married to a sailor who set sail from London one day and never came back. Not knowing whether her husband had died at sea, was a castaway or found a new life in some other place, the young mother raised the son the sailor had left behind.

Her situation turned dire when, about one year after her husband had vanished, she began to feel the first stirrings of another pregnancy. Of course the development could not have been a great surprise to her, but this did nothing to lessen her dismay. She had consorted with another man, but, protective of her honor in the eyes of her community, she had been careful to do so in secret. The thought of the shame she would endure if her husband's family learned she was expecting another child was enough to drive her from the city. Inventing a reason to depart, she left London and moved into an old friend's country home.

The young mother managed to stretch this friend's hospitality out for over four years, during which time she lost her one-year-old son to some sickness and gave birth to her daughter, Mary Read, soon after. Mary was nearly four when her mother decided that it was time to move back to London. Regarding the matter of her husband's family, she struck upon a plan. Seeing as how she had lost one child and gained another, there was no reason anyone had to know about her son's death, or, for that matter, her daughter's birth. She dressed Mary up as a boy, instructing her to answer to her son's name and conduct herself like any other healthy British lad. Mary must have been gifted at it, for in all the time she lived with her mother, no one suspected.

When she moved out of the house at 13 years old, she maintained the disguise, gaining employment as a footboy for a French family living in London. Perhaps it was force of habit, or maybe she had gotten to the point where she believed she actually was a boy, but Mary kept up the charade, even adopting a boy's ambitions and sense of adventure. She quickly became bored waiting on gentility and quit her job as a servant to join the military.

First serving in the Royal Navy for a number of years, she eventually joined the army, enlisting as a soldier in an infantry regiment. She saw much action in Flanders, where she distinguished herself as a brave and able fighter, earning the respect and admiration of every man who unwittingly fought alongside her. Whether or not it had anything to do with her corrupted upbringing, Mary seemed to take naturally to the soldier's life. Not just on the battlefield, either. Fierce in combat, she was free and easy in leisure, drinking hard and laughing lustily at barracks' humor. By all accounts, she was a "good-looking lad," lean and fit, with laughing eyes and a ruddy glow. No man thought for a moment, though, that there was a woman beneath the sharp angles of that military uniform. Not even the cavalryman she had become best friends with.

Mary took a strong liking to a Flemish horseman fighting alongside the British. For his part, the soldier was more than delighted when Mary revealed her secret to him, and the pair became inseparable. Who knows what the other soldiers thought of the very close relationship Mary and the Flemish man developed. Whatever rumors were circulating about the nature of the friendship were dispelled when Mary decided it was time to reveal that she was a woman.

Her desire to marry was what did it; knowing she would never be able to wed her cavalryman if the world thought her a soldier, she shed the burden of her disguise at her regiment's winter quarters, showing up on the arm of her fiancé with her hair down and fitted in a dress. The reception they received was overwhelmingly positive. There was the novelty of having a woman in their barracks. But this was nothing next to the realization that this woman had been one of their finest and most favored soldiers. When Mary announced their engagement, her comrades erupted in happy congratulations. They vowed that Mary would have the grandest wedding of any soldier in their regiment.

The wedding was indeed a large affair. Word spread quickly of the English woman in the soldiers' midst, and everyone with a saber or a rifle wanted to see her firsthand. Afterward, Mary was discharged from the service. With her husband, she opened a tavern called the Three Horse Shoes that did good business with soldiers. For a while, Mary enjoyed great happiness and may well have lived the rest of her days as a woman content in her marriage, passing anonymously into the currents of history. But this was not to be her fate.

Her husband died of illness shortly after they were wed. Then the Peace of Ryswick was negotiated, and the soldiers' patronage that had fed her business abruptly ceased. So it was that Mary was unhinged by capricious circumstance at the precise moment when she seemed to have found her place. She shifted back to survival mode, discarding her dresses and feminine fineries. She put on pants and a shirt, tied her hair back tightly and armed herself with a sword. Venturing back out into the wide world, Mary submerged her womanhood beneath a tough veneer, no longer a widow in mourning, but a carefree adventurer, an ambitious soldier of fortune ready to go anywhere.

In the early 17th century, "anywhere" meant voyage by ship, and after a brief stint in the military, Mary got onboard a Dutch West Indiaman and headed across the Atlantic toward the Caribbean. She was introduced to pirates for the first time in the lawless waters of the Bahamas, when a gang of freebooters looking for booty boarded the vessel. They were English robbers, who paid special attention to the disguised Mary because she was the only English sailor aboard the Dutch ship. Deciding that no self-respecting Englishman should be sailing under Dutch colors, the pirates took Mary aboard, pressing her into service without guessing for a moment that she was a woman.

And so began Read's life in the Caribbean as a cutlass-wielding swab, sailing under the Jolly Roger, plundering the freight of the civilized world. For a time, she alternated between stints at sea and periods of ease enjoying the fruits of her iniquitous labor in the taverns of Nassau. She came aboard Rackham's ship sometime after 1718, sailing as a privateer when Governor Rogers issued Calico Jack a letter of marque against the Spanish.

Despite the fact that she herself was a master of disguise, Read apparently did not guess that Anne Bonny was female. She must have been confused as she became the focus of Anne's attention. Everything clicked the night Bonny made her advance, when she hastily cast aside certain articles of clothing and telling anatomies were revealed. The discovery was an epiphany for both women, who hadn't realized the burden of their common deception until it was shed. Bonny and Read became devoted to one another, swearing to keep their mutual secret from the rest of the crew.

There were two men aboard Rackham's ship who discovered Read's identity. One of them was

Rackham himself. After the night they unveiled one another's deception, Bonny and Read spent most of their time together. No longer driven by romantic motivations, Bonny did not bother keeping her attentions to Read secret, not thinking how her newfound friendship would effect Rackham. Calico Jack, of course, had no idea that Read was a woman, only seeing that his mistress had developed a fascination for one of the younger men in his crew. In a jealous rage, Rackham confronted Bonny, assuring her that he knew what was going on and promising to make her lover into fish food. Bonny knew that Rackham's threat was serious. Seeking to avoid the possible death of Read, she let the livid captain in on the secret. Amazed and relieved, Rackham was good to his word and kept the news to himself.

The camaraderie between the two women saw expression in the business of piracy. In the following months, they became the two fiercest buccaneers aboard Rackham's ship, urging the captain to take on larger vessels, leading boarding missions, fighting with prodigious courage and cruelty. With two such fervent raiders in his crew, Rackham was not able to remain a legitimate privateer for long. They turned pirate with a purpose, plundering French ships off Hispaniola before moving on to Jamaica, where they attacked and robbed every ship they came across that was smaller than theirs, regardless of its nationality.

Bonny and Read were at the forefront of all these attacks.

Read surely enjoyed the pirating life as much as, if not more than, Anne Bonny. Rackham once approached Read about the obvious joy she took in her work. "What pleasure can ye possibly take from this occupation, lass, where by fire or by sword, life and limb hang in constant peril? To say nothing of the law, which, should ye be taken alive, will see ye strung up in disgrace."

To which Read gave her famous reply, "Cap'n, no straight-thinking seaman sailing under the black flag ought disparage the tradition of the gallows. In truth, we should be grateful for the hangman's rule. For if it weren't for the twine, then every cowardly fellow would turn pirate and so infest the seas, that sailors of courage such as ourselves would starve. Best not to wish away the hangman. Fear of him keeps most dastards honest. All those back home who make their living cheating widows, orphans and the poor would take to robbing at sea. The ocean would be so crowded with such cowardly rogues that no merchant would dare venture out. No, cap'n—let us not fear the dangers of our trade. For it is the fear of those dangers that make our livelihood possible."

And so they continued, seizing several merchant ships off the Jamaican coast, relieving the ships of their cargo and pressing some of their sailors into piracy. One of these newcomers had a dramatic impact on a certain woman in the crew. He was a sailor valued for some specialized skill—perhaps he was a cooper, or a cook or was adept at mending sails. Whatever his gift, he was less than thrilled to be aboard a pirate ship and did not get on well with most of his new shipmates. It was not long before he got on the bad side of one of the surlier pirates in Rackham's consort.

There were different ways to handle conflicts among pirates. Captains could be called upon to mediate issues, and it was not uncommon for punishments to be doled out according to traditional pirate codes. Failing this, sailors often resorted to fighting, angers diffusing in the aftermath of blackened eyes, broken limbs and swollen lips. But if a disagreement went too far, where a man's worth was called into question, then there might be only one resolution—a duel to the death.

The insults that passed between the newcomer and the burly pirate warranted nothing less than this final solution. The pirate made the challenge, and the newcomer had no choice but to accept. They would fight to the death by sword and pistol when they moored on the next island.

The fate of the neophyte buccaneer was essentially a foregone conclusion. No man aboard Rackham's ship believed that the newcomer stood a chance against his burly enemy, a skilled fighter and thief who had lived through many campaigns.

But since he had been forced aboard, the new sailor had come into possession of a trump that no one knew about. He had made a formidable enemy but had also befriended a powerful ally.

Almost nothing is known about Mary Read's relationship with this young man. Apparently it developed quickly, secretly and was intensely passionate. It was so much so that when Read learned of her lover's quarrel with the sailor, she took the first opportunity to find issue with the belligerent brute and challenged him to a duel herself. It was decided that this fight would also take place at their next moorage. Read insisted that she would not accept the possibility of her vengeance being denied in the event of her opponent's death in the other duel and so demanded that her fight take place first. No one guessed that she orchestrated this duel solely to save the life of her lover, who, she was certain, would not have survived the contest.

Mary Read faced her enemy when they came ashore on their next island. On a beach, in front of the whole crew, she fought for her life and the life of her lover. The fight was fierce and desperate. Read was the one who walked away. Her opponent was the one left lying on the ground clutching a mortal wound, his blood washing into the white sand.

Rackham and his crew continued on, raiding the waters around Jamaica until November 1720, when fate finally caught up with them. Once alerted of their presence, the Governor of Jamaica sent a ship after them, a large, well-armed sloop with a full complement of mariners. The Jamaican hunter rounded Point Negril, the westernmost tip of the island, and came upon Rackham's ship.

Rackham and his crew had just apprehended a small ship manned by a crew of nine English sailors. Not one hour before, Rackham had succeeded in pressing these men into service on his ship. After being plied with rum and promised all sorts of riches, they had agreed to join Rackham under the Jolly Roger and were given pistols and cutlasses for their new station in life. A celebration was underway when the Jamaican sloop appeared. The ship was close enough for Rackham's crew to see that it had been expressly outfitted for combat and was far better armed than their vessel.

Rackham shouted for all hands. The pirates jumped to their duties, weighing anchor, unfurling their sails, doing everything they could to escape the quickly gaining predator. But it was a lost cause. The Jamaican sloop was sleek on the wind. Soon within cannon range, it loosed a barrage at the pirates. With nine seaweed-green sailors who had never raised a weapon in their lives and a captain who was not the most determined fighter, Rackham's crew did not react well to the cannon fire. Men mumbled surrender as they half-heartedly executed their orders. Another round of fire and their resolve crumbled. They broke and ran for cover below deck.

In the end, it was just Mary Read, Anne Bonny and one other sanguine sailor who stood at the gunwales and exchanged fire with the sloop. When it became apparent that the rest of the crew, including Rackham himself, was content to cower below deck, Read and Bonny became enraged. The two women stormed to the hatch, shouting curses and calling out their comrades as cowards. Read went so far as to empty her pistols into the hold, killing one man and wounding a couple of others.

Three sailors willing to fight is no fight at all. Rackham's vessel quickly surrendered to the Jamaican sloop. They all laid down their arms and were taken into custody, including Bonny, Read and the nine Englishmen, who had not had a chance to so much as raise their cutlasses or steal a single doubloon from anyone. On November 16, 1720, they were brought before a court at St. Jago de la Vega. The grim sentence for Rackham and his crew was read: death by hanging. The hapless Englishmen who had never been given the chance to commit a single crime had to wait a few more months for their sentencing. When it came, they too were condemned to the twine.

There was nothing exceptional to the sentencing; 18th-century justice was typically harsh against piracy. Given Rackham's rather lackluster run at piracy, his passing may have been largely forgotten by history, just another dismal footnote in a turbulent time. But two shocking revelations at the hasty trial, secured the names Rackham, Read and Bonny in the annals of piratical legend.

The courtroom gasped when the judge asked the accused if any among them had anything to say about their sentences. Two slight pirates stepped forward, unbuttoned their shirts, and said: "Your Lordship, we plead our bellies." Both Read and Bonny revealed swelling stomachs and breasts beneath their shirts. It was obvious that they were women and that they were pregnant.

Thus Mary Read, who made the famous statement of being unafraid of the hangman's noose, ended up dodging it on account of her gender, which she had become so expert at concealing. So too, did Anne Bonny, whose plea of pregnancy instantly transformed her from a ruthless pirate into a delicate mother-to-be.

Not that the two friends enjoyed any great ending, continuing on as a pair of maidens-in-arms after clearing the shadows of the courthouse. Mary did not even make it to labor, dying of a fever while in prison, taking her unborn child with her. Bonny fared somewhat better. A number of Jamaican planters had been plantation owners in Carolina and had been friends with the rebellious girl's father. She was given her freedom and was even given permission to visit Rackham in his cell on the day he was to be hanged.

Her soon-to-be-former lover was in an understandably bad state. Bonny gave him what comfort she could, uttering the notorious words of consolation that would become the famous conclusion of her legend. "I'm sorry to see ye here like this, me dear," she said, a gentle hand on his back, "but if ye'd fought like a man, ye need not have been hanged like a dog."

No one knows what became of Anne Bonny or her unborn child.

CHAPTER SIX

The Wretched Edward Low

Thus these inhuman Wretches went on, who could not be contented to satisfy their Avarice only, and travel in the common Road of Wickedness; but, like their Patron, the Devil, must make Mischief their Sport, cruelty their Delight, and damning of Souls their constant Employment. Of all the pyratical Crews that were ever heard of, none of the English Name came up to this, in Barbarity.

–Captain Charles Johnson, 1724

As LOATHED AS BLACKBEARD was for his violence and cruelty, he was also in possession of certain characteristics that leant him something of a romantic air. Brutal as he could be, he was also a famously courageous sailor who would gladly meet his enemy in combat, no matter how desperate the odds. His seemingly bottomless avarice drove him to a life of constant robbery, but when it suited him, he also had a penchant for unusual generosity. He frequently rained gifts upon his North Carolina neighbors between expeditions.

Perhaps most importantly, Blackbeard was a master of theatrics. With bright ribbons tied into an enormous beard, smoking fuses under his hat and the hysterical script of hyperbolic chauvinism he was wont to spout, Blackbeard understood the aesthetics of swashbuckling better than anyone. His demeanor was often so extreme, it was as though he was consciously writing his own legend while he was still alive. Though Blackbeard was a murderer, a thief, a womanizer and a drunkard, at the very least it could be said that he pursued these dissolute passions with enough theatrics, color and flair that future generations could make him into a kind of romantic figurehead—a raving anti-hero of a violent and tumultuous time.

The exact same cannot be said of Edward Low. A butcher whose staggering acts of violence were adorned by nothing but a brazen psychopathy, Low was lost at sea without a moral compass, a man in a position of power without a shred of human decency. In the period known as the "Golden Age of Piracy," Captain Edward Low was as close a thing to the devil as could be found in the waters of the "New World." The men who served under him were prodded into becoming the demons of his own floating hell.

Perhaps he was born this way. Coming from a rough family in Westminster, Low terrorized his way to the top of his school's hierarchy. He did not learn to read or write and became aware of his own bottomless sadism by tormenting the local boys for the change in their pockets. When he was too old to make his living this way, Low went to sea.

Natural born bully that he was, Ed appears to have taken his time applying his talents at sea. He spent some three or four years in legitimate trade. Sailing the shipping lanes across the Atlantic, he no doubt fit in fine with the less savory set of sailors. There is no record of anything that would foreshadow the depravity of the coming years.

He eventually settled on land, working in a Boston shipyard, where he earned a modest living as a laborer in a rigging house. In the few years he worked on the waterfront, Low suffered from ever-increasing issues with authority, frequently coming into conflict with foremen. He finally gave up on the grueling work and took to the water once again.

This time, he was on a sloop bound for southern waters, through the Caribbean and into the Bay of Honduras, where he worked as a logger. Low, by this time an experienced seaman, did not do any logging himself. He was given command of a shallow, 12-man boat that transported the lumber from the mainland to the larger ships anchored off the coast.

It was not easy work. Laborers were forced to contend with the heat, the exertion and the constant threat from the Spaniards, who viewed English logging in their territory as nothing less than outright theft. Because of the threat from the Spanish, Low and his 12 men were always armed with cutlasses and pistols while on the job. There was an unremitting tension to the entire operation, like a military campaign behind enemy lines. The difference was that the rootless young Honduras loggers did not have the structure of military discipline or a national mission to give shape to their conduct. In the vacuum of such disciplinary forces, Low's brutal alpha personality quickly came to dominate the 12 sailors manning his boat.

Low tended to get along fine with the men subordinate to him but had a serious problem with authority. His last tenure as an honest workingman was terminated on account of this problem. It happened at the end of a particularly grueling day, when Low and his men, exhausted and hungry, pulled alongside the freighter just as the evening's meal was being prepared. They were sure they had made their last run of the day.

"A blight on this damned heat," Low said, leading his exhausted men onto the deck of the ship, their mouths watering at the smell of cooking fish.

"Drain me through the bilges," one of his men said. "If I don't get food in me, I'm liable to take a bite out of someone's arm."

That was when the captain of the ship stepped down from the poop deck to where Low and his men were slumped. The captain wore a little bit too much weight around his belt and was sweating under the sun's last rays. "What's this, Low? No rest yet. We intend on departing at first light on

the morrow. There's room for one more load in
our hold. You and your boys still have one more
round to make."

There was visible dismay on the faces of Low's
men; a few of them were already turning back to
their boat. Low, however, did not move. There was
a dangerous light in his eyes and his jaw had set
into an ugly grin. "Ahoy, I hadn't realized ye were
made admiral, matey," Low said. "But even if ye
were the damned Queen, I'd tell ye me hearties
aren't setting foot on that boat until we get some
grub."

The captain had been dealing with Low for the
last few days and so was not completely surprised
by his reply. Sighing, he called for rum. An instant
later, one of his men handed him a full bottle. The
captain turned to Low. "Take this, man, and get
yourselves back on that boat for one more trip.
There's no more time for these pleasantries."

Without changing his expression, Low snatched
the bottle of rum with one hand and pulled his
pistol with the other. "Much thanks for the generosity, admiral," Low said. "Now let me repay ye."
The captain shouted in alarm and fell back on his
heels just as Low pulled the trigger. Fortunately
for the captain, he tripped at the moment the pistol was discharged and so dodged the ball. The shot
flew across the deck and embedded itself in the
skull of a hapless sailor, killing him instantly.

Chaos erupted on the ship as some men dove for cover while others raced for weapons. Low and his men raced for their boat, exchanging fire with the crew as the ship's deck became thick with gun smoke. Somehow, they made it safely to their boat and heaved off into open water without any of them suffering a single wound.

They sailed directly out of the bay, continuing through the night until they came upon a ship that was only slightly larger than their own. There was little deliberation over what to do next. With Low leading them over the bulwarks, they boarded the vessel, taking ownership of ship and cargo and forcing the crew onto the smaller boat. Watching the frightened crew make their hasty getaway, the loggers made a black flag from tattered cloth and, as Captain Johnson so eloquently put it in his grand history, "declared War against all the World."

Thus, with 12 loggers and a tiny vessel bobbing over blue Caribbean waters, Edward Low began his infamous and wholly corrupt career. He and his men sailed to the northeast for the Grand Caymans, mooring in Georgetown around Christmas of 1721 to outfit their humble little vessel and consider their next course. There they met a scoundrel named George Lowther, captain of a good-sized ship called the *Happy Delivery*, whose aims were not so different from their own. Lowther was an English sailor who had recently gone pirate, in charge of a good-sized crew and with no short-age of ambition. He took one look at Low and rec-ognized the danger simmering beneath the surface. Here was a man who was attached to nothing and dear to no one. Not only rootless, but also unhinged, capable of anything. In short, exactly the kind of man a pirate captain wanted in his crew. Lowther ended up taking the loggers onto his own ship and appointed Low his lieutenant.

Lowther's plan began with a westward jour-ney. It was back to the Bay of Honduras for Low and his 12 sailors, officially on the account of George Lowther, now among leisure-loving, idle and mostly drunk pirates, instead of the angry and overworked loggers they had come down with. If the 12 loggers were sometimes uncertain about their new careers, Low had no such doubts. He had found his calling. Second in command aboard the *Happy Delivery,* he was only obliged to take orders from one man, Captain Lowther. And even then, he would not take the captain's orders for long.

Lowther and Low had great fortune cruising the Bay of Honduras. Arriving on January 10, 1722, they promptly spotted a 200-ton merchant ship from Boston called the *Greyhound.* The ship offered a stiff resistance before surrendering to the pirates, for which the crew was stiffly punished. After the surrender, when the pirates came aboard the *Grey-hound,* they immediately set upon the crew. Blood ran freely over the deck of the captured ship, as every man was clubbed, whipped or cut before being thrown into the brig of the *Happy Delivery*. Then, after they relieved the *Greyhound* of its valuables, they put the ship to the torch. It is not known who gave the order to torture the captured men, Lowther or Low—either way, the needless bloodshed foreshadowed Low's love for senseless torment and mutilation.

The devil continued to smile on the *Happy Delivery*, which continued its profitable cruise through the Bay. They captured two brigantines from Boston, one mid-sized Connecticut sloop, another from Virginia and yet another from Jamaica. They also captured a 100-ton sloop from Rhode Island, which Captain Lowther put in Low's charge. The pirates had sailed into the Bay of Honduras in one ship, but they left as a modest fleet of four sloops. There was no denying this was a great start, and spirits were high. But it did not last.

Pushing into the Gulf of Amatique, they found what they believed to be safe ground for careening and counting of the spoils. There was a lot to count, and the treasure was brought to the beach by the boatload, along with sails and rigging in need of repair. The mood was lively as the men went about cleaning hulls and counting gold. Then disaster struck. It burst from the jungle without warning. There was a thunderous whoop and shout, and then hundreds of natives came crashing out onto the beach with weapons raised, their intentions obvious.

Thrown into a panic, the pirates floundered for what possessions they could carry before splashing for their boats. They rowed frantically for those ships that had not been heeled, crowding towards the largest remaining sloop as the natives on the beach began plundering their ill-gotten gains. All at once, the prosperous fleet had been reduced to a penniless rabble packed onto a single sloop.

They departed from the Bay of Honduras short on provisions, in a vessel too small to accommodate them and with nothing to show for months of raiding. They sailed east, toward the Leeward Islands. The high morale that so recently marked the expedition crumbled, replaced by general misery. Idle in their cramped conditions, the crew soon gave in to bitter reprove, each man blaming the other for their state of affairs.

The situation might well have deteriorated into anarchy if they had not come upon the next prize when they did—a brigantine, of good size, off the island of Deseada. There was no deliberation or hesitation. Setting their course to intercept without even bothering to appraise their quarry, the pirates were fortunate that the brigantine was not a warship, for given their desperation, they likely would have attempted to board it, regardless. As it was, the brigantine was lightly defended. Low's crew had little problem capturing it and plundering its cargo. Their long-simmering discontent finally found an outlet. After stripping the ship of its goods and crew, they put it to the torch, bellowing in joy as the symbol of their misfortune sank to the ocean bottom.

Heartened by the encounter, they set sail for northern waters with a plan to plundering the Atlantic Coast. This was as far as Low went with Captain Lowther. They had reached the 38th Latitude on May 28, 1722, when they spotted a good-looking brigantine plying the water. The vessel surrendered without a fight, and once he and his men had boarded, Low made his ambitions clear. He had no intention of sailing under Lowther's colors any longer. He would take this ship under his command and captain his own crew. Any man who wanted to join him was welcome.

The move was no surprise to Lowther or his crew. The captain and his lieutenant had been disagreeing regularly. When things became desperate after they left the Bay of Honduras, the crew split into two feuding camps—one under Lowther, the other under Low. While the divisions had mostly healed since then, the memory of the rift was still fresh. Low was able to use it to realize his own ambitions. As for Captain Lowther, he did not dare speak against his rebellious lieutenant. He could see that the danger that once simmered inside of Low was about to boil over, and he had no wish to be there when it happened. The two parted company in those waters. The crew split almost exactly down the middle—roughly 40 pirates went with Low, and roughly 40 remained loyal to Lowther.

ther did not fare well after parting
tégé. In June, he won a series of
ries, capturing three or four fishing
one small sloop off the coast of New
then, sailing south, he was thoroughly
trounced in an engagement in South Carolina
waters when he was outmaneuvered and his ship
badly holed by his prey. He and his crew were
forced to limp into a North Carolina inlet, where
they spent the winter repairing their ship and
recovering from their wounds. And Lowther's
luck turned out to be far worse in 1723. After
spending the spring in Newfoundland, bullying
humble ships of little account, Lowther headed
south back to the Caribbean. Here he was greeted
by more of the same misfortune, sailing for
months without a single prize, eventually capturing two tiny vessels, both of which yielded nothing but sorely needed provisions—no treasure.

The end came to Lowther in October. Ordering
his grumbling crew to careen the ship on Isla la
Blanquilla, an unpopulated island some 100 miles
north of the Venezuelan coast, Lowther was taken
completely by surprise at the sight of a southbound sloop approaching. His sails, rigging and
cannons had already been pulled to shore for the
cleaning, so he was completely helpless as the
sloop changed direction to approach Lowther and
his crew. A vessel careening in some out-of-the-
way island usually meant one thing: pirates. And
this sloop's captain was not about to pass up the

opportunity to capture a ship of robbers. Lowther's men did the best they were able, pulling their ship ashore in a desperate attempt to save their one way off the island, but without cannons or sails, they were powerless when the sloop opened fire. Pirates scattered for cover as the artillery rained down on the beach. When the attacking ship sent its boarding party, only five members of Lowther's crew were found. They were taken aboard the sloop as prisoners. The pirate ship was hastily re-rigged and transported to the mainland.

Once informed of the engagement, the Spanish Governor sent out a search party for the remaining castaways on Isla la Blanquilla. They captured four more men, but George Lowther was not one of them. None of them could say what happened to the luckless pirate. Some time later, his corpse was found on the beach by a passing ship's crew. It was believed he shot himself, as he was found alone, without a trace of any other man, a discharged pistol by his side.

Ed Low and those pirates who accompanied him fared much better. Better in a manner of speaking, perhaps. While most of them had greater success in their plundering of the seas, there is no accounting for what mark Low's freakishly cruel methods left on their souls.

Low's terrible tenure as a pirate captain began on June 3, 1722, off the waters of Rhode Island, when he boarded a sloop from Amboy, New York.

He was quite civil about his first robbery, taking the provisions off the ship and then sending the crew on their way without any harm. The second prize came later that same day, a ship heading into port in Rhode Island. Low stripped this ship as well and ordered the rigging and the sails to be cut, so as to prevent the ship from sailing in and raising the alarm. He took insurance by cutting off a number of the master's fingers to delay repair.

On July 12, Low pulled a daring stunt, sailing straight into the harbor of Port Roseway, raising the black flag and capturing the 13 vessels moored there. The maneuver was such a surprise in its audacity that no one was able to mount any sort of defense. Before the day was over, Low's ravaging crew boarded every one of the anchored ships, emptying them of everything in their holds. Low also took command of the largest ship there, an 80-ton schooner that he named the *Fancy*. One of his favored sailors was put in charge of his brigantine. They pressed several of its crew into signing Low's articles. By the time they weighed anchor and sailed from the port, Low's outfit had swelled to two ships and 80 men.

Low soon decided it was time to head back for southern waters and gave the order to set sail for the Leeward Islands. They did not get there before enduring much trouble, however. They sailed into the Caribbean just in time for one of the worst tropical storms that summer. It was a raging tempest, turning the waters around the Leeward Islands into heaving, roiling ranges of nautical chaos, waters curling and crashing in avalanches of roaring foam. The storm only got worse as it moved west and was a full-fledged hurricane by the time it hit Jamaica. Roughly half the buildings in Port Royal and 40 docked ships were laid to waste, while over 400 people lost their lives.

This was the storm that Low's two ships found themselves in while sailing south. It came very close to ending the crews' piratical reign of terror. Taking in massive amounts of water, both ships had pumps and bailers working continually day and night. Not drawing out enough to keep up with the enormous waves washing over the bulwarks, the ships began to founder. The captains were forced to consider radical options; ballast and then provisions were thrown overboard to keep the ship afloat. Arms, powder kegs, fresh water and food were all pitched overboard in turn. At one point, when the storm was at its zenith, Low even considered tossing his mast and sails into the water.

But both schooner and brigantine managed to ride the storm without resorting to that desperate measure. Separated in the storm, the vessels found each other after it cleared. Battered and sorely in need of provisions, they were floating in the waters north of the Leeward Islands. They found a small nameless island where they moored to take stock of the damage.

It was determined that the schooner had suffered greater damage than the brigantine and needed some time for repair. But Low was not about to let a damaged ship quell his ambitions. Ordering every remaining weapon moved onto the brigantine, he also stocked the ship with his best men and what provisions they were able to secure from local natives. Thus an undeterred Low set out for plundering while his schooner was being repaired.

The expedition was no great success, rendering only one captured ship, a victim of the storm that was drifting helplessly and struggling to reach Antigua without mainmast or sail. Low boarded the merchants without a fight, taking everything of value and leaving them in the condition in which he had found them. Importantly, on this short-lived expedition, Low discovered that the Leeward Islands were not safe for cruising, being crowded with patrolling naval vessels. He returned to the island when his schooner was repaired, a new plan in mind.

They would not go any further into the Caribbean but head in the opposite direction, toward the Azores—the name given the nine islands in the North Atlantic that had been colonized by the Portuguese. Up until this voyage, nothing Edward Low or his crew had done would have branded them with a murderous reputation. They had enjoyed relatively good fortune in the number of prizes they had taken. The raid on Port Roseway had been daring enough to win them some recognition. They had committed occasional cruelties, but nothing that was so beyond the piratical pale. That was until they journeyed to the Azores.

Did something happen to Edward Low during that long journey over the waters of the Atlantic? Was it some perverse progression in the captain's mind, born from bad company and too much rum? Or perhaps it was a sickness that he nursed, a psychotic inner dialogue that he festered over in his cabin. Or, could he possibly have been a murdering maniac all along, only expressing his bloodlust once he had arrived at the Azores? Whatever the case, it was in the waters around this small cluster of islands that Low's bloodthirsty nature first became dreadfully apparent.

The raids began civilly enough—or as civilly as one could ask of a ship of pirates. Before boarding a ship, Low made it a point to announce that anyone resisting his crew was condemning everyone on the ship to certain death. Low had much success with the approach, making the threat with such gusto that no one dared doubt it. The pirates took many ships without so much as firing a shot. Those crews that cooperated were usually allowed to continue on their way after they had been stripped of their cargo. But there were some exceptions.

One of his prizes, a converted man-of-war called the *Rose,* he kept. He stocked it with guns and took command of it himself, passing the command of his schooner on to the captain of the brigantine. In another case, Low did not like the looks of the cook on a French ship he captured. Evacuating the entire crew except for the cook, who he ordered tied to the mainmast, Low explained that the man, being a "greasy fellow," would fry well in the fire. With that, he set fire to the ship with the screaming cook bound onboard.

On August 20, Low's flotilla came across a galley whose captain disregarded Low's threat. His crew found the courage to put up a fight against the pirate ships bearing down on them. And they paid dearly for it. When the freebooters finally maneuvered alongside the galley and boarded, they were in a murderous frenzy. With Low shouting for retribution, they charged on to the galley's deck, cutlasses drawn and blood in their eyes.

The crew of the galley immediately surrendered, but this did not spare them from the pirates' fury. Low and his men took their time, spending the next few hours drinking rum and murdering and torturing at their leisure. They hacked off limbs, ears and digits. They disfigured some of the men with fire. Low had always spoken of an extreme personal dislike for the Portuguese. He was most pleased to discover a number of them on the ship. There were two Portuguese friars, in particular, who he ordered strung up by their necks from the foreyard arms. Coughing and spluttering, the two monks were raised and lowered several times before being strangled to death. Another Portuguese passenger, weeping openly at the slow murder of these two revered men, was disemboweled by cutlass.

In the midst of the rum-filled barbarity, one small punishment was dealt against Edward Low for his brutality. It was a case where the punishment hardly fit the crime, but Low would carry the mark of it for the rest of his days. This dram of justice took the form of a misplaced cutlass blow from one of Low's pirates. This man, his weapon raised over an unarmed prisoner, was drunk beyond basic coordination. He missed his target with a mighty, if completely imprecise, swing. Captain Low, who was standing nearby, was the one who received the edge of the blade.

The cutlass sliced Low's jaw open, leaving a gaping wound that revealed the bottom row of his teeth. The ship's doctor was immediately called up to look at the writhing, swearing captain. A bottle of rum was prescribed, and the doctor began stitching Low's face back together. The problem was that the physician was about as sober as the rest of Low's crew, and the end result was not as well executed as the captain hoped. After taking a look at the doctor's work, Low vehemently expressed his disgust and received a fist across the chops for it. The doctor, hardly the model of Hippocratic compassion, hit Low in the exact spot that he had been cut. He broke most of the stitches, condemning Low to a hideous scar that remained with him for the rest of his days. That the captain did not kill the doctor right there on the spot speaks volumes of how valued men of medicine were on ships of the day.

The same respect was not afforded to the galley's crew. After the pirates grew tired of bloodshed, they took everything of value and cut all the sails and rigging. They then set sail, leaving the bleeding crew stranded in the middle of the North Atlantic.

Next was a voyage south to the Cape Verde Islands, a cluster of 15 islands some 400 miles west of Africa that had also been colonized by the Portuguese. Just as in the Azores, Low conducted his "civilized" pattern of pillaging, winning several prizes by hoisting the black flag and issuing the ugliest threats he could think of. No one dared to stage any kind of defense, and so the raids around Cape Verde went easily enough, with no recorded atrocities.

This is not to say that Low's expedition to Cape Verde was not tinged with failure. While his pirates had grown quite adept at boarding and stealing from other ships, they apparently had not mastered the procedure of careening. While taking the time to clean the barnacles off Low's man-of-war, they overset the ship at its careenage, rendering it unusable. Thus Low was forced to retake command of his old schooner, the *Fancy*, now packed full with about 100 pirates, the crew of two ships.

He considered trying a stint of terrorizing the coast of Brazil, but after losing a small scouting fleet he had sent out to gather intelligence to that end, Low decided it was time to head back to the Caribbean. They had just set sail for western waters when they came upon a well-appointed Portuguese ship called the *Nostre Signoria de Victoria*. Lowe did not hesitate for a moment. The order to intercept went up and down the ship, and all hands came to deck. After a brief exchange of fire, Low's men were aboard the vessel, tearing through the holds looking for treasure. Finding nothing but a spare cargo and basic provisions, they then began to extort the crew, demanding to know the whereabouts of their booty. For there was no doubt that such a rich-looking ship should be carrying at least some treasure. Disaster came when one of the sailors, pressed by torture, confessed that they had been carrying a bag filled with 11,000 Moidores, but that the captain had dropped this enormous treasure into the sea just before they were boarded.

A Moidore was a valuable Portuguese gold coin; 11,000 Moidores was a fortune. The thought of this fortune lying on the ocean bottom brought out the worst in Low. With an eruption of a thousand oaths, Low had the captain tied to the mainmast. He lit a fire at the captain's feet and, pulling his knife from his belt, cut the captain's lips off his face. Low cooked the lips over fire, sprinkled them with salt and pepper, and forced the bound captain to eat them. Only after he had swallowed the last grisly morsel did Low pull his pistol and shoot the captain dead.

Hardly cowed by Low's barbarism, his men hooted their encouragement. Their captain gave the final order of the engagement. "Kill them all! Each and every one of them!" And so it began. Low's men were diligent in their execution, going to work with cutlass and pistol, leaving not one of the 32 Portuguese sailors alive. The luxurious *Nostre Signoria de Victoria* was turned into a blood-soaked blot on the Atlantic.

By the time they returned to the Caribbean, Low and his men were changed men. The nightmarish acts they had committed in the Atlantic clung to their sails and hung with ineffable weight from the rigging, casting a pall over the character of every one of them. They were no longer just pirates but had become butchers, remorseless devils, murderers capable of anything, upon the inaptly named *Fancy,* a plane of hell on the water. But they did not immediately reveal their viciousness in the Caribbean. Capturing several vessels among the Leeward Islands, Low and his crew were quite well behaved and limited their wrongs to theft and sporadic violence.

It was not until mid-March 1723, when they arrived in the Bay of Honduras, that they let the devil out of the box. The victim was a Spanish sloop that was coming out of the bay. Spying the vessel, Low had his men hoist up Spanish colors and then gave the order to approach their unsuspecting quarry. Only when they were within shouting distance did the *Fancy* pull down its false colors and raise the black flag in its stead. Low fired one broadside at the Spanish ship before boarding it with all hands. The Spanish surrendered before any blood was shed, not knowing the sort of men they were surrendering to.

Perhaps things would have gone smoothly if it were not for the five prisoners Low's men found in the sloop's brig—five Englishmen, each of them a captain of his respective ship, which the Spanish sloop had captured on a successful excursion just that morning. Perhaps Low was suddenly reminded of how menaced he was by the Spanish when he himself had been an English logger in the Bay of Honduras. Or perhaps the occasion was nothing more than an excuse to put on a false patriotism and indulge himself in another massacre.

Whatever the case, upon hearing the English prisoners' stories of defeat and capture at the hands of the Spanish, Low exploded into a rage. He turned to his men and gave the order. What they had done to the Portuguese aboard the *Nostre Signoria de Victoria*, so too would they do to the Spanish here. Thus the massacre of the 70-some Spaniards began—as horrific and chaotic a scene as can be imagined. The unarmed Spanish did their best at self-preservation on a cramped deck, while over 100 pirates went about their brutal work, shooting, stabbing and clubbing their victims to death. Some Spaniards jumped overboard to avoid the killing floor of the deck, but Low was bent on exterminating them all and called on a handful of men to pursue by boat. Those who attempted to escape to the coastline were killed before they got there—bludgeoned with oars or shot while they swam. Only after the last man was cut down did Low's crew search the blood-soaked sloop, taking the riches for themselves and setting fire to the ship. The ship went to the ocean bottom. The wash of blood in the water and charred planks were the only signs that it was ever there at all.

After setting four of the English captains free—one, being a carpenter, was considered too skilled to be let go and was pressed to sign the articles—Low gave the order to return to the Leeward Islands. There they cruised for some time, back and forth between the Lesser Antilles and the Venezuelan coast, where they captured several more ships. These vessels were mainly Jamaican and English. There is no record of any depravities visited on their crews.

This may have been the last time Edward Low cruised the Caribbean. The next time he appeared to the civilized world, it was May 27, 1723, off the coast of South Carolina, where he spread mayhem. It seems that the Portuguese were not the only sailors he detested. A New England vessel's entire crew was tortured. Low personally cut off the captain's ears and nose before letting the ship go on its way. On another vessel, also from New England, Low ordered his men to tie matches between the sailors' fingers and light them on fire, burning their tissue to the bone. Several ships from London and the southern colonies were plundered as well. None of these suffered the evils visited on the New England vessels.

These depredations did not go unnoticed. A Royal Navy man-of-war called the *Greyhound*, with 120 disciplined sailors, 20 guns and a determined Captain Peter Solgard at its helm, was informed of the brutal pirates sailing north. Cruising the waters around Rhode Islands in search of the wretched company, Solgard met up with Low's two ships on June 10, and the battle was on. Low came on strong, seeing Solgard's one vessel to his two and not yet knowing he was facing a determined hunter who was ready for a fight.

The captain of the *Greyhound* played to Low's confidence, feigning a retreat and drawing his zealous enemy into an engagement they were sure they would win. This put-on chase went on for about two hours, until the *Greyhound*, finding herself in a favorable position, suddenly swung to face the oncoming ships. Both Low and his consort raised the black flag and loosed volleys on the warship, perhaps believing that a quick surrender would follow.

Instead of dropping sail and yielding, the *Greyhound* unfurled its mainsail and caught the wind, showing its broadside and returning fire at close range. Only then did the pirates understand what they were facing. They went no further but turned and clapped with the wind, suddenly in a running fight. The man-of-war was on them for roughly two hours, gaining steadily until they pulled in for a close exchange of cannon and musket fire. Outnumbered and outgunned as the *Greyhound* was, military discipline kept the soldiers at their guns. Low's consort had its rigging cut to ribbons and its main yard blown apart. As the *Greyhound* pulled alongside the crippled ship, Low shouted for all hands at the rigging and guided the *Fancy* out of the cloud of powder smoke and away from the battle. If Low had turned around, then, and come to the aid of his beleaguered comrades, the two pirate vessels could have easily defeated their foe. But in the moment when it counted, Edward Low, who had no issue maiming and murdering unarmed prisoners, did not have the nerve to turn and engage a determined enemy.

While Low got away that day, his second ship was captured after a brief fight. Twelve pirates of the lost vessel were killed or fatally wounded. Captain Solgard took the rest prisoner, delivering them to a Rhode Island courthouse. On July 19, the 35 sailors were tried in colonial court. Twenty-five of them were found guilty and executed that same day.

In a rage, Low took his defeat out on men he was far more comfortable confronting. Off Rhode Island, he captured a Nantucket whaling ship. He cut the captain's ears off before shooting him through the head. He loaded the rest of the crew on one of their boats, gave them only the barest provisions, set their ship on fire and then departed, leaving the whalers at the mercy of the sea. He visited similar carnage on a number of other ships. He decapitated the master of a fishing boat off Block Island, about 10 miles south of the Rhode Island coast. The captain of another whaler was disemboweled and cut to pieces. Yet another captain had his ears cut off and was made to eat them.

And so it went. Low's temper seems to have cooled somewhat when he made the decision to sail north to Newfoundland. The waters were rich with prospects. Low's crew thrived, capturing over a dozen French ships off Cape Breton and something close to 20 vessels on the coasts and harbors of Newfoundland. Having lost nearly half of his company in the Rhode Island engagement, Low was quick to increase the size of his crew. He forced captured sailors to sign his articles and converted the larger, more seaworthy vessels into pirate ships.

By the end of July, a week or so after the sailors he abandoned to the *Greyhound* were executed, Low was in command of a three-ship fleet. He made up a new ensign for this refurbished fleet—a red skeleton stitched on a black flag—and set course for the Azores and then the Canary Islands. All the while he remained faithful to his calling of theft and butchery, leaving death and misery in his wake.

There is no clear account of what became of Low. It is known that he captured and outfitted another ship off the coast of Africa. The sailor who was put in charge of this vessel, one Captain Francis Spriggs, deserted Low's fleet at first opportunity and sailed his crew back to plunder the more familiar waters of the Caribbean. Low captured one last ship in January 1724, but he then falls from the pages of history.

It is said that he was planning an expedition to Brazil, but no one can say whether or not he ever made it there. Some put his ultimate fate at the bottom of the ocean, his fleet coming on a storm in the Atlantic and sinking with all hands. Other versions have him succumbing to his own crew, who mutinied after he killed his quartermaster in a homicidal fit. In these accounts, Low was put on a boat in the middle of the ocean and was eventually discovered by a passing French warship. He was taken to the island of Martinique, where he faced a court and was hanged for his crimes.

Whatever his fate, after January 1724, there is no record of any other ship suffering carnage at the hands of the Caribbean's cruelest pirate. He passed into history without love or mourning. His legacy amounted to little more than a mound of dead and maimed sailors and a narrative of cowardice and barbarity.

Notes on Sources

Carlova, John. *Mistress of the Seas*. New York: The Citadel Press, 1964.

Cordingly, David. *Under the Black Flag: The Romance and the Reality of Life Among the Pirates*. New York: Harcourt Brace & Co., 1995.

Defoe, Daniel. *A General History of the Pyrates*. New York: Dover Publications, Inc., 1999.

Earl, Peter. *The Pirate Wars*. New York: Thomas Dunn Books, 2003.

Exquemelin, A.O. *The Buccaneers of America*. New York: Dover Publications, 2000.

Jameson, A.B. *Naval Adventures & Buccaneers*. New York: Brunswick Subscription Co., 1910.

Klausmann & Meinzen. *Women Pirates & the Politics of the Jolly Roger*. Montreal: Black Rose Books, 1997.

Lucie-Smith, Edward. *Outcasts of the Sea: Pirates and Piracy*. New York: Paddington Press, 1978.

Mitchell, David. *Pirates*. London: Thames and Hudson, 1971.

Pyle, Howard. *Buccaneers & Marooners of America*. London: T. Fisher Unwin, 1891.

Ranklin, Hugh. *The Golden Age of Piracy*. Williamsburg: Colonial Williamsburg, 1969.

Dan Asfar

Dan Asfar has a flare for writing lively narrative, evidenced by the strength of his first popular book of history *Outlaws and Lawmen of the West: Volume II.* Asfar also is co-author of biographies on the famed Metis rebel leaders Louis Riel and Gabriel Dumont. Dan, who has a degree in history, has authored nine other books of non-fiction, travelled extensively across North America and has visited Australia and Mexico in recent years, all in pursuit of regional folklore.

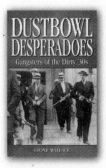
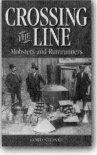